The Human Side of Quality and the
TAO: The Greening of Leadership

Draft Version

Harry,
Best Wishes
Michael

P.S. Clean Version to Follow

By Michael R. Basso, Ph.D., MBA,

1

Expanded Contents

About the Author

Dr. Basso has significant experience as a leader in quality and reliability engineering and management in industry, as well as being a college level educator in psychology at Yale University and the University of Connecticut. His experience also includes being a consultant, researcher, and newspaper columnist. Michael is the president of the Connecticut Holistic Health Association.

Dr. Basso has a Ph.D. in professional psychology and biomedical systems, an MS in engineering science, and an MBA with a focus in executive leadership and an interdisciplinary Professional Development Diploma in pathophysiology, neural systems, and education. He also holds a BS in electrical engineering. Michael is certified in quality and reliability engineering and quality auditing, as well as variety of health related areas.

7

Preface

This innovative book is meant to provide a broad integrative overview of quality concepts from a bio/psycho/social/techno/spiritual perspective, with due consideration for cultural diversity, individual differences, and planetary responsibility; as well as individual and social wellness. With the internet so readily available, much of the extensive background information commonly found in earlier leadership texts was purposefully left to the reader to research. The latest information about a topic of interest can also be found readily on an as needed basis.

This *abbreviated* approach provides a practical, roadmap for the truly innovative leader and aspiring employee alike, given the time constraints common in productive organizations. The book is ideally suited as a text for *leadership* seminars and workshops, as well as graduate level academic courses.

It is expected that the creative leader will be led to think of the bottom line in a much broader context than before reading this book. It is also anticipated that the innovative leader will at first use what is relevant to them personally as well to their organization. From a solid foundation, they could springboard into whatever future *continuous improvements* are useful and relevant at later times.

Some of the core constructs associated with this book were written twenty years ago, as my MBA thesis in international business, from an executive leadership perspective.

One of the most difficult aspects of preparing to write that term project was choosing the topic. When the paper is a thesis level project the difficulty is proportionally magnified, as would be expected; especially when you decide to go way above and beyond the schools requirements. Given this dilemma I chose a topic that would touch upon key subjects that I had studied in all of the graduate courses and many professional seminars. My goal was to integrate these aspects with viewpoints gained from personal experience and, more importantly, through personal aspirations regarding the way I believe quality system plans should be developed and implemented.

Relevant concepts from cognitive, social, clinical, developmental, cultural, I/O, health, and political psychology, medicine, neuroscience, organizational development, business management, negotiation and decision sciences, and communications have been seamlessly integrated with quality management concepts.

The generic concepts described can be specifically tailored to apply to any type of organization established in either the private or public sector; including manufacturing, educational, healthcare and just about any other type of organization with goals and objective.

When reading about the cases, the reader is advised think about related situations, even if your organization is focused in different arenas. The basic concepts are the same; it's only the surface variables that change.

The purpose of this book is not necessarily to replace the quality system that works best at your organization, but to provide insights that are expected to facilitate the *improvement of the improvement system* itself.

Prologue

Quality can be related to any system that has specifications or goals, whether physical, technological, scientific, educational, or managerial in nature; and is a measure of how well a system meets these specifications and goals. The system is said to be reliable when these requirements are met over time and / or different environments or circumstances.

Innovations such as the Holistic Quality System and the Greening of Leadership are seamlessly integrated with concepts from Professional Psychology and Organizational Development.

The Quality of the employees themselves and of their leadership is key to the quality of everything else. Holistic Leadership is broad in nature and considers the integration of best practices from a variety of disciplines, including bio-behavioral, technological, environmental and financial.

The Human System is a comprised of a composite bio/psycho/social/spiritual being that is programmed by nature for optimal survival, effectiveness, and efficiency. As the human system reaches the optimal state of homeostasis, losses are minimal, while gains are focused within the constraints imposed by nature, the culture they belong to, and the financial, human and technical systems they interact with.

Holistic Organizational Quality Systems

Planning and implementation of an integrated systematic approach designed to: understand the perceived expectations of our internal and external customers; monitor and feedback the status of humanistic and technical subsystems; and facilitate enduring corrective actions focused towards continuous improvements, constrained by profitability and balanced by maximizing the health and happiness of the employees while minimizing losses to society and negative ecological impact.

Michael Basso, Jr. 1990

PART I

History and Systems of Quality

Introduction

The evolution of the *Total Organization Quality System* throughout the twentieth century has been an inevitable survival characteristic of organizations being molded by powerful forces both internal and external to the organizations. Analogous to biological organisms, many organizations are evolving through the stage of continuous homeostasis towards the stage of continuous improvement. I propose that the next evolutionary step will be the continuous improvement of the *holistic organization quality system; with a focus on the humans leading and implementing the system.*

Ongoing improvements include, but go beyond the concepts promulgated by the present quality gurus. This includes J.M. Juran's concepts of *fitness for use* and *quality system planning*; W. Edwards Demings' *14 Points for quality management* (including constancy of purpose towards improvement, ceasing of dependence on inspection and heavy emphasis on team work); Arman Feigenbaum's subsystems *for total quality control* (such as preproduction quality evaluation, extensive quality training and post production quality service); Philip Crosby's *14 steps for quality improvement* (including top management commitment, cost of quality evaluations and quality improvement recognition systems); Kaoru Ishikawa's *total quality contro*l (including emphasis on top down

14

management leadership, bottom up total employee involvement and entire product life cycle quality coverage) and Genichi Taguchi's emphasis on the *practical use of designed experiments* and the *quality loss function*. Later innovations, including *quality function deployment*, *policy deployment*, *software quality assurance* and *documentation quality* are just the beginning.

Any organizational system, including the global approaches, such as *Kaizen*, *Six Sigma and Lean*, could be improved by a deeper understanding about the human system within the quality system, within the organizational system, which is anchored within the social system.

I propose that holistic organizational quality systems will go beyond the realm of *profit maximization* into the domain of the *maximization of employee health, happiness and fun*. Environmental forces will force human organizations towards the systematic and continuous process of ecological quality improvements. This will go much further than mere compliance to regulatory limits. One might conclude that the evolution of the *bio/psycho/social/techno/spiritual* model proposed will be constrained by individual differences and cultural diversity. Due consideration for *individualist* versus *collectivist* sociocultural background is paramount for successful implementation of the new quality system.

Among the internal cultural indicators that an organization has an effective quality system are: an internal and external customer orientation, a teamwork approach to problem solving and rewards and a preventive strategic approach towards avoiding problems. Less quality oriented organizations are typically; management driven, reactive and focused on short range, high impact fixes with questionable duration and further improvement required.

To facilitate a large scale organizational change focused towards quality improvement the commitment of top management is foremost. The commitment itself however is predicted by and proportional to the perceived tangible and intangible benefits associated with implementing the quality improvement system.

The purpose of this part of the book is to describe key factors, both academic and practical; that cause organizations to change their quality systems; the processes involved in planning and implementing these changes; and the short and long term results expected.

An evolutionary approach will be used from both the historical and strategic perspectives. The beginnings of modern quality science from the efforts of Mr. Shewhart at Bell Labs and those of Dr. W. Deming will be explored. Japanese contributions will be explained throughout this paper from the massive

16

national study and training efforts leading to the development of *quality circle* team problem solving, after WWII, to the evolution of the modern *Taguchi methods* for designing quality into products and the *Kaizen* factors for the continuous quality improvement. Implications of the international quality standards and political interventions will be discussed.

The strategic factors of quality planning and policy development will be complimented by the control * aspects of audit, inspection, feedback and corrective actions focused upon goods and services from both the internal and external customer perspective.

Due consideration is giving to the planned strategic transformation into time oriented tactical innovation and continuous improvement.

An integrated approach was used to explain the synthesis of the traditional quantitative statistical aspects of quality technology with the humanistic behavioral aspects of quality systems psychology from both the individual and the organizational perspectives. Shall we begin?

*Quality systems can be separated into two broad categories: Quality Assurance and Quality Control. Quality Assurance pertains to the "planned systematic actions necessary to provide confidence that a product or service will satisfy given needs." (ANSI/ASQC A3-1978)

Quality Control pertains to "the operational techniques and the activities which sustain a quality of product or service that will satisfy given needs; also the use of such techniques and activities." (IBID)

Benefits Derived From Implementing a Holistic Quality System

Highly Tangible benefits include

> Profits increased by more than the cost of quality implementation
> Increased market share
> Decreased advertising costs
> Decreased production liability costs
> Reduced absenteeism
> Decreased employee turnover
> Decreased product development time

Less tangible benefits include

> Employee happiness
> High levels of employee health
> Customer satisfaction
> Decreased loses to society due to waste
> Minimized ecological impact
> Responsible fun
> Peaceful working conditions
> Joyful employment

Select Characteristics of Poor Organizational Quality Systems

Poor Quality Orientation

Reactive Approach

Short term Corrective Actions that do not last

Top down Management

Driven by Customs

High Impact, Short Term Improvement

Individual Objectives

First Come First Served

Point Indicators versus Ranges

Blame Oriented

Secrecy Oriented

Hero Oriented

Time Not Considered

Select Characteristics of Good Organizational Quality Systems

Strategic Quality Planning

Participative Quality management

Integrated Quality Orientation

Preventive in Nature

Continuous Process Improvement (Kaizen)

Group and Individual Objectives Well Integrated

Priority Driven

Statistically Valid Indicators

Solution Oriented

Communications Oriented

Team Oriented

Human Waste Minimized

Lean / Time Optimized Processes

Initial Japanese Contributions to the Quality Sciences

When I was a small boy, in the 1950's, Japanese toys were usually considered to be low quality *junk*. The perception of these products was often so bad that children would make a mockery of kids having Japanese toys. Today the tables have certainly turned. The 'Made in Japan' stigma has turned into a symbol for reasonably priced, high integrity products.

This metamorphosis was spawned by the political transition towards industrialization after World War II. The historical aspects of initial Japanese contributions will be described in this section. Recent advances in the field of design quality will be explained in the section on New Product Quality.

In the Beginning

The first phase of the plan was for key players to systematically study the quality programs used abroad. To facilitate this study, Q.C. *study teams* were initially formed from the ranks of upper management, quality middle management, college professors and technical specialists. The next wave of trainees were foremen and the other first line managers. The works of U.S. quality experts, Dr. W.E. Deming and Dr. J.M. Juran, were among the most prominent studied. The emphasis at this stage was on *online quality inspections* and subsequent analysis using the simple statistical techniques such as:

Pareto Analysis
Frequency Histograms
Scatter Diagrams
Control Charts

By 1950 the trainee had become the trainer. Organized by the <u>apanese Union of Scientists and Engineers</u>, one of the most penetrating training programs in history had begun. A faculty of teachers was employed to start at the top and teach statistical methods thru the vertical strata of industrial hierarchy. The training was so extensive that the national radio network was used to supplement the in person training with courses given over the air six days a week. By the mid 1950's, the Japanese began creating their own innovations in the fields of: reliability, new product development, operations research, computer data analysis and *cause and effect analysis*.

In the realm of cause and effect analysis, the works of Dr. Ishakawa, including the famous Ishakawa (fishbone) Diagram, are noteworthy.

The Next Step: Quality Circles

By the early 1960s, the simple statistical ideas imported by Juran and Deming were becoming transformed into Japanese quality systems. The most well known of these systems is the *quality circle.*

A quality circle is a *participative management system* where participants meet at regular intervals to discuss, analyze and solve quality problems. Each circle has a leader, usually a supervisor or technical leader. Several circles are coordinated by a *facilitator*. The facilitator also assumes the role of trainer and supporter. Several facilitators are managed by a *steering committee*. The steering committee sets the policies and procedures for the programs and acts in a mediary function with other management functions.

The system caught on like wildfire. By 1972 over 5 million documented Q.C. Circle projects were completed with estimated average yearly savings of about $5,000 per product.

Socio-political and Behavioral Transitions Inspired by the Post WWII Quality Revolution

The success of the Japanese began to be perceived as economic and social threats to other industrialized nations, including the United States. In response to these threats the organizational change theories of behavioral and social scientists began to take on a new and vested significance[1]. The purpose of the next three sections [2] of this book is to explain academic and applied socio-political and behavioral mechanisms relating to organizational changes, and individual responses, inspired by the *international quality revolution* developed after WWII. The Japanese were continually inspired to improve their organizational systems, stimulating further U.S. improvements, ad infinitum.

---

1 A hidden benefit of the "Quality Revolution" has been to inspire funding of Organizational Development Research.

2 (Strategic Quality Planning and Policy Deployment, Societal Factors Effecting Quality System Planning and Humanistic Aspects of Holistic Quality Systems.)

Strategic Quality Planning and Policy Deployment

Top management must perceive the need to make a change before such a widespread change as the development and implementation of a *holistic quality organization* is likely to occur. According to Lewin's Change Model (17) the level of behavior of an organization is the result of forces striving to maintain status quo and those pushing for change. Forces driving quality changes external to the organization, and no under it's direct control, include; *economic*, such as loss of market share; *technological*, including innovations in the quality sciences; *political*, such as the announcement of an international quality award; and *social*, such as the need to minimize scrap (and maximize the utilization of natural resources). *Environmental scanning* (7) is a systematic method for organizations to monitor and forecast these external forces. Within the organization, information must be fed to the internal political making group[3] (42), from credible sources, indicating the need for quality improvement (i.e. decreased profits, impending product recalls, or safety issues). Quality improvement 'champions' would benefit most by engineering the communication to the *motivational* stimulating characteristics (28) of the top management

---

3 The Policy Making Group would typically be comprised of top managerial decision makers, be formalized in procedure and focused towards the establishment of meaningful high impact communications.

audience. Information would be used to *unfreeze* the matrix holding present organization patterns in place.

Policy statements are used to define general 'rules of conduct,' to be followed throughout the organization, to facilitate the goals set forth in the mission statement. To gain commitment it's important that key managers participate in the policy development process. The resulting policies must uniquely define the organizations history, management and state of development to maximize impact (14). Such policies as; "commitment to running hospitals with the safest emergency room procedures in the state" or "growing the highest quality fruit in the industry," are examples of general policies.

The organizations philosophical value statement is used to establish the relationship between the organization and its stakeholders[4] (7). Values such as; respect and dignity for stakeholders, commitment to "pack the customers dollar full of value"[5], quality and satisfaction, and the promotion of continuous innovation[6] are examples of organizational values.

---

* Cognitively motivated managers would tend to be motivated by facts and figures, while socially motivated individuals are motivated by humanistic values, etc.

---

4 Stakeholders include employees, customers, shareholders and suppliers.

5 Taken from the philosophy statement of J.C. Penny Co., Inc.

6 Taken from the value statement of Pitney Bowes, Inc.

It takes much more than passing out wallet cards packed with mission, value and policy statements to change the quality culture of an organization. A sound comprehensive communications strategy is needed to promote organizational cohesiveness (14, 28). To maximize effectiveness, the strategy should; elaborate on *historical accomplishments*, including the experiences of quality heroes; use quality leaders as role models to be emulated (this helps establish a feeling of *oneness*); establish the relationship between job security, reward systems and training, to quality (this tends to promote a sense of *membership* within a quality oriented organization); and promote *exchange* between all employees and quality oriented managers (staff meetings and participative decision making, and inter-departmental offsite social events are examples of exchange mechanisms.) Powerful communication media used to promote quality concepts include newsletters, video tapes, posters and brochures. To be effective, any significant reengineering effort had best take into consideration the intrinsic and extrinsic motivational drivers of all important players.

The next step in the quality strategic planning process is to set long range (with a horizon greater than one year) *strategic objectives*. The objectives are to be compatible with the organizational *culture* and *climate*, be *realistic* and *attainable*, and be *capable of being measured*. They should match the organizations strengths with opportunities (i.e. utilize behavioral scientists from R&D to participate in writing the charter for a new human resources quality department); minimize threats to the organization (i.e. develop a corporate quality system to increase the market share of product X by 10%, with a 90% confidence level); and eliminate weakness in the organization (i.e. train all employees in statistical process control by December 2011. Short term objectives, created to be compatible with the long term ones, are filtered through the lower strata of the organization).

Among the special concerns related to setting quality objectives improperly, I'd like to discuss four that I find to be particularly important; setting the same quality goals arbitrarily *for all products* in a business unit, setting objective standards without soliciting the *customer view point*, emphasizing *individual objectives as opposed to group objectives* and neglecting rewards for slow but steady continuous process improvements.

It does not make sound economic sense to allocate the same level of quality improvement funding to improve an unproductive 'dog' (7), about to be divested, as would be expended on a dependable 'cash cow'. Product maturity, inherent design capability, and present level of quality attainment make each product unique. Unique product quality goals are both practical and fair, but unfortunately uncommon.

Quality objectives set without customer orientation are typically inefficient, costly, impractical and often absurd. The analogy of setting the paint finish standard for a rental bulldozer the same as that on a customer owned Rolls Royce will hopefully drive this point home. Unfortunately many western companies do not get this point very well.

Systematic approaches, including internal and external customer surveys and quality function deployment[7], can be useful for setting rational workmanship and functional standards. A particularly useful method of using surveys is to use correlation analysis to quantitatively relate customer satisfaction to specific parameters. Standards can be prioritized accordingly.

During the early part of this century, Dr. J. E. Deming promoted the denouncement of emphasizing individual objectives as a major contributor to costly internal competition. The Japanese took heed and the rest is obvious history.

Kaizen (36) is a Japanese word that means continuous improvement in all areas of personnel and work life. The Kaizen approach to quality improvement emphasizes *long-term, long-lasting effects*, opposing the western orientation towards short lived dramatic innovation. The Kaizen system emphasizes typically

---

7 QFD is discussed in the section regarding new product development.

non dramatic, but consistent, change and team involvement versus short lived glory for individual heroes. The point is that unaccommodating reward systems need to be upgraded to include recognition for the accomplishment of 'Kaizen type' dependable objectives.

Organizational structures must be correlated to strategic objectives to assure their fulfillment. Symptoms of the need to change organizational structures include (7):

Excessive decision making at the top
Overworked key personnel
Excessive meeting frequency and number participants

These *quality indicators* are key points to be considered by the quality organization during the organizational audits conduced at both the corporate and functional levels, including the quality *sub-organization* itself. To assure objectivity, audits of the quality organization are best conducted by auditor's independent of the quality organization, such as by the internal audit group or an outside consultant. Note that first and second level organizational structure groupings (i.e. function/function or function/products) have been correlated to inherent characteristic problems regarding competitive response, market response and internal functions (7). These findings can be used as a guide to help understand and correct functional problems.

One of the most potentially powerful ways to deploy quality policies is, in my opinion, to hire innovative corporate staff vice presidents of both quality and human resources (a carefully developed and synergistic relationship can help to assure that both the technical and humanistic aspects of quality policy are developed and deployed as to maximize effectiveness). At the next level down, line quality directorships, in such areas as financial, marketing, R&D and design engineering, manufacturing and customer service, can be powerful strategic players used to rapidly infiltrate the functional organization as participative planners and implementation watchdogs.

Short term quality objectives must be correlated to the strategic quality objectives and fit to the organizational structure. The specific plans to fulfill these objectives are best developed *participatively* with the applicable functional groups. The use of planning controls, such as *milestone charting, critical path method* and *Pert charting* are useful to help assure timely and efficient planning and implementation. Supportive documentation such as a *quality manual* containing business unit standard operating quality *policies*, and specific quality *procedures* must be carefully maintained and reviewed at least as often as objectives are set to assure the maintenance of correlation and relevance.

Although I haven't seen any literature regarding the subject, I think the topic of *quality oriented budgeting* is worthy of discussion and serious investigation.

The budgetary procedures of an organization are typically the most prevalent form of control in an organization. (7) Unfortunately, they're also one of the potentially most disruptive mechanisms used to thwart quality objectives. Too often management will avoid the implementation of quality objectives. Too often management will avoid the implementation of a quality policy because the budget will not allow it. *Inflexible budgeting* doesn't account for the unexpected costs inherent when an organization is 'stirred up' by the implementation of an organization wide quality program. Perhaps *zero based budgeting*, which is <u>not</u> built from the previous years budget would buy a little more flexibility. Better yet would be a budgeting system based on a model that considers statistical projections (with specified levels of confidence) based on previous failure trends and distributions, the anticipated impact of quality system changes and a safety buffer reserved for non random special events. Perhaps the proposed system could be named the *statistically based quality budgeting system.*

The strategic and short term organizational changes discussed in this section should not be considered to be *refrozen* (17) indefinitely. Remember that the quality improvement process is a continuous one. Those employees used to *skating* on a solidly frozen *organizational pond* better carefully test the ice before skating on their old track marks once the quality improvement process has begun in earnest.

Societal Factors Effecting Quality System Planning

Organizations that produce products and services can be considered to be an integrated body of subsystems that are externally influential by social, technological, political, regulatory, economic and environmental factors.

As a result of tension from the other general *societal* factors, and prioritization established by political orientations, organizations are explicitly influenced, directly by regulation and indirectly by standard procedures and policies.

Government regulatory bodies, international quality standards, and *national awards and conventions* have a profound influence upon the planning, implementation and control aspects of total organizational quality systems.

In Japan, nonconformance to specifications are contrived to be losses to society from both the cultural and the quantitative perspectives.

In all societies, besides international competitive factors, it makes sound economic sense to improve the quality of all a nations' goods and services. From a macroeconomic perspectives, funds wasted on scrapped or reworked products, with associated tax benefits, can contribute to inflation by diminishing the relationship between funds paid for and products provided. For everyone in the plants benefit, the efficiency of the utilization of our *limited natural resources* needs to be maximized to ensure our future survival. Recycling and other green management practices are important aspect of the quality culture. Due consideration for practical, safe and effective *stress leadership programs* are also an important aspect of the holistic quality system.

Regulatory Agencies and Legislation

Most industrialized countries have governmental and professional regulatory bodies chartered to assure that products and services conform to national quality standards. Among the most critical function of the quality assurance department is to assure that; product and process specifications specify the applicable standards (while designating the respective governing agencies), and that program plans provide for testing appropriate to prove compliance.

Governmental agencies that regulate quality standards (including state and local levels) include, but are not limited to, functional criteria, compatibility criteria, health, safety criteria and additional *quality of work life* [8] criteria.

---

[8] QWL legislation will be expounded upon the Quality of Work Life section of this paper.

Examples of functional regulatory agencies would be the Institute of Electrical and Electronic Engineers (IEEE), the Universal Postal Union and the American National Standards Institute (ANSI).

Safety standards would include regulation by; Underwriters Laboratories (UL), The British Standards Institute (BSI) and the National Safe Transit Association (NSTA).

Compatibility with other users is regulated by the Federal Communication Commission (FCC), legislation, sections the FAA legislation, and the National Illumination Society Standards.

Note that the price to pay for nonconformance to some regulated quality standards can be greater than anticipated program profits. Any organizational quality system that doesn't include watertight plans to assurance conformance is potentially courting direct financial penalty and indirect negative public opinion.

International Quality Standards

To assure *consistency* of workmanship, measurement and comparison, standard controlled documents are often utilized[9]. *Primary* standards are at the head of the standard documentation hierarchy. The next level of more specific standards (based on the primary standards) are called *secondary*, which are followed by *tertiary* standards, and so on down the line. Note that a common requirement of quality systems is that standards are *traceable* to the Primary standard. For example, calibration procedures for assembly line test equipment are required by the British Standards Institute to be traceable to the National Bureau of Standards.

The primary international quality standards were developed by a Technical Committee 176 of the International Organization of Standardization[10]. Called the *ISO 9000* series, five standards were published in 1978. (25) ISO 9000 is the guidebook for the series. ISO 9001-3 standards document three levels of generic external[11] quality management

9 It's of primary importance that quality oriented organizations have quick access to and/or a repository of applicable up to date quality standards

10 ISO has more than; 176 technical committees, 648 subcommittees, 1606 working groups and 26 ad hoc study groups, representing 73 national bodies and a membership of greater than 20,000 experts from around the world.

Note that technical committee 56 of the International Electrotechnical Commission (IEC) is instrumental in the development of reliability and maintainability standards.

11 External quality documents typically refer to relationships between purchasers and suppliers.

planning and implementation strategies. New ISO standards are in process which relate to comprehensive auditing, service quality, process, measuring procedures and software issues.

These standards have been adopted by most industrial countries and have spurred the development of *National* primary standards. (These would be secondary to the ISO standards.) Based on the national standards, hundreds of military and industrial standards have been generated. The quality system standards hierarchy is often stratified in iterations down to product specific workmanship standards which can be as specific as to define accept/reject criteria regarding scratches and dust. In fact, in 1988 more than 11,000 quality related standards had been published in China. (35)

In the United States, the American National Standards Institute and the American Society for Quality Control have developed the ANSI/ASQC "2" series, focused on sampling plans and procedures, and the ANSI/IEEE software quality standards.

As an integral part of the European Community *EC 1992* economic improvement strategy, the ISO 9000 series has been adopted. In addition, each EC nation has developed a standardized audit and registration scheme for the evaluation of manufacturing companies. Among the leading countries to adopt this system is the United Kingdom, with more than 10,000 registered companies in 1989. (The U.K. Has also developed national standards called the BSI 5750 series - for evaluation manufacturing systems).

Germany, France, Norway, and Denmark are also leading advocates of quality system evaluations. Italy and Spain have non-governmental membership societies similar to the ASQC. (22) Extensive government intervention is underway in the Netherlands via the ministry of Economic Affairs. (The results of a national survey conducted in 1989 [5] has revealed the only 16% of the 98 Dutch countries surveyed had written quality policies and only 25% had quality managers)

The USSR has adopted ISO 9001, 2 and 3. They've developed their own version of ISO 9000 and ISO 9004.

In China, during 1988, the China State of Bureau of Technical Supervision (CSBTS) was established to merge the State Bureau of Metrology, the State Bureau of Standardization and the Bureau of Quality Control. Additionally in the same year legislation was passed, by the seventh National People's Congress to regulate industrial quality standards by the government. (35) (Incidentally, during the Qin Dynasty [221-206 BC] the emperor Qinshihuang established measurement standards by imperial edict)

Japanese quality standards are primarily governed through the Japanese Industrial standards Organization (22). Manufacturers apply for certification and authorization to use the (JIS) mark on their products. The insignia is mandatory for products involving consumer safety and voluntary for other products. This is certainly testimony to the premise that the honor system can work quite well in the appropriate culture.

National Quality Awards

Several nations have adopted the policy of bestowing government endorsed awards to outstanding contributors to the National Quality Effort. Note that these wards are considered very prestigious and that they often have a profound impact on public and commercial relations for the recipients. Among the most noteworthy awards are the Deming Prizes in Japan and the Malcolm Baldridge Award in the United States.

During the 1950s the Deming Prize Award Committee was established in Japan. The committee included quality science authorities from the government, academia, industry and the press. Three prestigious awards are bestowed upon organizations based primarily on quantitative improvements in quality and productivity.

The Deming Prize is awarded to individuals and teams that have made noteworthy contributions in the field of theoretical quality sciences and technology. Dr. Genihi Taguchi, a prominent Japanese statistician, is one of the most famous recipients.

The Nikkei Quality Control Literal Prize is awarded to outstanding individual contributors to any area of quality control literature.

The Malcom Baldridge National Quality Award

During the early 1980s, the United States government was goaded by the threat of the loss of the international leadership role in terms of product and process *quality* and *productivity*. This condition was further aggravated by the fact that in 1985 Japan was becoming the top creditor nation in the world, while the U.S. was becoming a net debtor nation. Conversely, it was becoming widely accepted, by the U.S. Legislative body, that a national quality award would help improve quality and productivity by; formally *recognizing* the achievements of outstanding companies, establishing guidelines and criteria to help other organizations improves, and to provide specific guidance to organizations willing to learn how to improve their quality outputs. These conditions, in combination with impetus given by the American

41

Society of Quality Control (ASQC), the National Advisory Council for Quality (NACQ), the National Productivity and Quality Center (APQC), led to the submission of House Bill 5321 "to establish a National Quality Improvement Award" (and the later related documents - House Bill 812 and Senate Bill 1251). The fruition of these efforts was realized in August 1987 when former President Reagan signed the Malcolm Baldridge National Quality Improvement Act. (9)

The award conceived from these efforts is jointly managed by the National Institute of Standards and Technology (NIST) and the Malcolm Baldridge National Quality Award consortium. Funding is managed through the Foundation for the Malcolm Baldridge National Quality Award.

The Board of Examiners is organized with 9 judges, 28 senior examiners and 100 examiners. The assessment criteria are distributed among seven general categories, with 33 subcategories, divided into 62 specific items.

Note that the Canadian government has established a Canadian National Quality Award, which is very similar to the Malcolm Baldridge Award.

National Quality Months and Years

In addition to National Quality Awards, some countries have endorsed National Quality Months which emphasize quality education programs, speeches and contests.

In 1984 former President Reagan, in cooperation with ASQC and the U.S. Congress, proclaimed October to be National Quality Month for the Unites States. The Canadian national government and all 10 providence governments have also proclaimed October to be their National Quality Month. (2)

Great Britain, Czechoslovakia and Yugoslavia have declared National Quality and Reliability Years. The year starting October 1966 was chosen by Great Britain. (22)

The Quality Loss Function

The traditional, particularly western, viewpoint regarding functional specifications is that as long as the parameter in question is within its specified tolerance limits it's considered to be acceptable, and no further consideration is warranted.

In Japan, this discrete (go/ no go) approach to functional quality is considered, at best, to be simplistic and short sighted. The *Quality loss function*, developed by Dr. Genichi Taguchi, promulgates the concept of a continuous quantitative loss function. The degree of deviation from specified target values, caused by *noise factors*[12], is related to losses incurred by society.

The qualitative aspects of the loss function can be extended to consider variation losses as contributing to scrap, rework and recalls (due to preference for *on target* parameters and the probability of a quicker degradation to *out of spec* conditions for parameters initially farther away from the ideal specified condition. The Japanese consider the economic and cultural implications as extending throughout society.

---

12 Noise factors can be subdivided into: <u>outer</u> noise factors, such as environmental variation and human error; <u>inner</u> noise factors, such as deterioration; and <u>between products</u> noise factors, such as manufacturing imperfections. Ideally, products should be <u>robust</u> against these factors, which tend to cause product variability. Noise factors are also outside of the controlling aspects of the design product of process function. (See Exhibit S3)

44

Some western quality philosophers are starting to think likewise, more 'taoistically'.

Human Resources Aspects of Holistic Quality Systems

It is my firm contention that the *right brained* humanistic aspects of total organizational quality systems are among the potentially most rewarding frontiers that will (or should be) explored during the next century.

Special consideration must be given to the human resource functions of an organization to assure that quality system plans are humanistically developed and transferred into viable and productive cultural changes, standard operating procedures and objectives. (I've coined the term *human resources transfer function*[13] to describe this process). The HR transfer function would also be needed to assure smooth implementation with diplomatic control processes. [14]

Organizational development interventions in the area of *quality of work life* (17) changes and legislation can also be considered to be a sub category of the humanistic aspects of the quality sciences.

---

13 The human resource functions include; employee acquisition, integration, development, maintenance, and renewal.

14 See Exhibits H1 through H3

To maintain consistency, human resource quality practices need to be documented as standard policy, which is auditable by the quality department. It may be organizationally sound to create a human resources quality department. (I am not aware of any presently in existence. I bet they'll be commonplace in the next century.)

Acquiring Employees

Recruiting, screening, selection and placement of employees is critical to the success of the organization.

To improve the *quality of the acquisition process*, the *structured interview* and *application process* can bring in the right human capitol for the job at hand.

References from *trusted internal employees* may also be significant for bringing the right employees into the quality oriented organization.

In order to assure the proper fit among work groups, informal tactics may also be used by the recruiter to ascertain *biodata*, such as interests, hobbies and other relevant aspects of background information.

Armed with information about the new employees' *skills, knowledge, accomplishments* and interests, the well trained recruiter may be the most important quality leader in the organization.

The training of the recruiter would ideally include aspect of both the quality and organizational sciences to assure appropriate fit with the *primary* (those whom they hand out with) and *secondary groups* (the formal employer/ employee relationships) that she/ he will be working with to fulfill the organizations mission.

Integration of Employees

The orientation of employees into quality focused organizations could realistically be extended to include a *tour of duty* in the new employee's functional *customer's* department, prior to or shortly after, commencing a new job. In many Japanese companies, designers are required to spend as long as a year in manufacturing and customer service departments before they're entrusted to design products. In the U.S. this wide spread neglect of this practice has had devastating effects in terms of impractical and un-manufacturable designs.

I think the concept needs to be extended further in both the east and the west. For example, if marketers were required to spend time in engineering departments, learning engineering concepts and terminology, more meaningful customer surveys

48

could be developed. False promises, in terms of unrealistic delivery times and unfeasible designs, could also be minimized. All primary suppliers would benefit from productive time spent in customer service and quality departments. The need becomes even more pronounced when the customer relationships are made more complex by foreign transactions.

The same arguments can be made for healthcare, educational, and municipal organizations, with just a change in variables.

Maintenance Functions

The Human Resources Information System (HRIS), whether manually or computer driven, can be utilized to keep track of employee participation in quality training programs, professional quality certifications (i.e. ASQ certified quality or reliability professionals.)

Continuing medical education (CME) activities, teacher recertification training and time at the range for police or first aid training for firefighters is equally relevant for improving the quality of the organization.

Matching Objectives to Needs

The match between individual objectives and individual motivational needs is often neglected. This mismatch would tend to diminish job satisfaction as well as efficient and cost effective problem solving. Ideally, various testing instruments could be used by the functional managers after being trained by the human resources training department. The purpose would be to determine the factors that *motivate* departmental members as well as to assess their *task-related potential*.

For example, those departmental members that are *motivated by esteem* would logically find tasks leading to high responsibility and recognition to be rewarding, while those individuals striving for *self-actualization* would need to work on challenging tasks that require high levels of creativity and which would afford opportunities for career advancement. Due consideration for *extrinsic motivational factors*, such as *expectancy* and *equity* must also be realized. (42, 59) The human resources department would need to train the functional managers accordingly.

The less tangible benefits of these motivational interventions might be more impressive however. A high quality of work life would lead to *happier, healthier, employees, more satisfying customer relationships, and hence, in the vein of Dr. Taguchi,*

50

would minimize losses to society. This would be a true *win-win* situation for both the organization and the collective market.

Environmental Concerns

The working environment can have profound physiological as well as psychological impact on people, which in turn can impact productivity, quality and hence profits. Environmental factors such as quantity and spectral characteristics of lighting, the ergonomic design of furniture, the color of the walls, the ionization of the air, can be designed in such a way as to facilitate creativity, *minimize errors* and *reduce absenteeism*. Studies from both academia and industry abound which substantiate these claims. The human resource departments could be instrumental in spearheading task forces designated to assess the costs, *projected benefits*, and viability of this too often neglected aspects of a total quality system. The guidance of an experienced *outside consultant* could certainly be useful here.

Renewal

Changes can be quite disruptive to any organization in terms of the implementation of new technologies and the management of significant changes.

The systematic solution to often random and unpredictable problems is one of the primary crosses for organizational quality systems to bear. To be effective, problem solving techniques must include an organized approach to solving problems that provides for; effective problem definition, installation plans for problem solving technologies (these are often of a foreign and complex nature to users), and end-user ownership. (43)

Problem definition must be *clear, concise and focused* in such a manner that both management and end-users perceive tangible benefits from the solution of the problem. Otherwise commitment is unlikely. In fact, one of the basic rules of problem solving teams is to define a formal *problem statement* before any work is focused towards solutions. I've seen this approach effective used often to refocus divergent, and much wasted, problem solving energies.

Installation plans for quality technologies are more effective if they're built on *previous successes*. This approach can break down barriers from the commitment of supporting management. In my opinion, one of the greatest concerns for quality system installation is that *contingency plans* be established in case the primary plans go wrong. (One of my greatest frustrations as a quality professional has been to have material flow managers blame the quality department for assembly line shut down, when in fact the production control system was working with no contingency buffer. Prematurely installed *just in time* systems can wreak more havoc than most people would imagine.)

End-users must feel ownership if they are going to use the quality system techniques installed in their functional areas. If they are given the *choice* to participate in the planning process changes, they'll alleviate some of the *not invented here* problem typically found when quality departments force their ideas on the functional end-users. Freedom of choice requires that the end-users are given the knowledge (43) about the quality technology being utilized. This is both an implicit and explicit function of the quality department.

One of the most tragic consequences of installing quality system interventions in a company is the *emotional stress* imposed on both the change innovators and those being changed. In a holistically oriented organization, the hidden aspects of the *cost of quality* calculations might include the costs of psychological and physiological impact vs. the degree of product or process perfection*.

Even less enlightened organizations would benefit from the development of a stress diagnostic system (20), including surveys and psychological/physiological testing; a stress prevention system which includes fitness and nutritional programs; and a stress management system (41).

Select QWL Interventions

Quality of work life (QWL) programs can be considered to be a labor and management cooperative approach focused towards the mutual enhancement of organizational productivity and employee well being. This element of a total quality program emphasizes *participative problem solving,* including quality circles*, working committees and dedicated task teams; work design efforts (4Q) geared towards improved meaningfulness of work, increased accountability and autonomy, and timely and appropriate feedback; innovative *share the wealth rewards systems*, such as the Scanlon, Rucker and

---

*quite possibly some innovative mathematically oriented behavioral researcher may someday develop a "stress impact function" based on the probability of inducing stress vs. the degree of product imperfection allowed.

Impro-share plans (12); and *environmental* improvements**, including improved lighting and ergonomically designed work areas, flexible working hours, nutrition and fitness programs and *self-managed work groups.*

Work Design

At the turn of the 20th century Frederick Taylor, an engineer turned steel executive, designed a work system called the *scientific management* system.

He considered workers to be extensions of machines that should be treated as interchangeable parts. The system stressed top down communication and virtually ignored employee contentment and informal communications. It is my position that the word scientific is a true misnomer describing Mr. Taylor's system. Much of the social and behavioral scientific viewpoints were missing from the equations.

Most employees tend to be more productive when they perceive their jobs as meaningful, when they feel responsible for their destiny and when results are *fed back* to them.

*See section regarding Historical Japanese Quality Milestones.

**See section regarding HR Maintenance functions.

Meaningful work is associated with *skill variety, task identity and task significance*. When several skills are involved in a job, the *de-motivating* factor of monotony is lessened while the job becomes more challenging and interesting. When a worker completes a whole project, as opposed to a perceived unconnected subassembly, they can more easily identify with their work. Task significance is related to the perceived impact of their jobs on the organization and society. It has been my observation that subassembly inspectors tend to be more restless, Collectivist versus Individualistic Considerations less happy and they tend to make more mistakes, than final product inspectors.

The degree of *job autonomy* is related to personal responsibility. Worker freedom, independence, and the ability to determine how to do one's own job are the factors that determine autonomy. Feedback must be relevant to what was actually done and must be given in a timely manner to be effective. (I can personally attest to how bad it feels to have a performance review held up. I once had a promotion held up for 6 months. The retroactive pay didn't balance the feelings of uncertainty about getting the promotion and the perception that my boss wasn't very concerned about my feelings.)

Gainsharing Reward Systems

Gainsharing reward systems are those where participants in cost savings improvement projects are remunerated by a percentage proportional to the operating results enjoyed by their company. Gainsharing system designs are more successful and readily accepted when they are developed cooperatively between Unions and Management representatives from a cross section of the company. The size and organizational structure of the company must be considered regarding the domain of the plan and the consideration for instituting multiple plans. The determination of bonuses must be considered regarding what proportion should go to the company and what percentage would go to the employees. The frequency of the bonus payout determination is constrained between optimal timing for employee motivation and company profits. Effective plans should be dynamic systems managed by a <u>cooperative</u> steering committee that's responsive to needed changes.

One of the earliest and most prevalent gainsharing plans (*The Scanlon Plan*) (17) was developed in the 1930's by Joe Scanlon, a Union Leader, who strongly believed that managers and *labor* should share information, problems, goals, and ideas and that that goals of workers should be coincident with the goals of the organization. The major emphasis of this program is to enhance productivity with associated labor cost reductions. All organization members participate and regards are distributed equitably. Employee suggestions are reviewed by a management/labor production committee.

Rucker plans (12) are similar to Scanlon plans; however the suggestion process is usually coordinated by a management appointed *idea coordinator*. The bonus formula is extended to include cost and savings associated with production and material purchases and inventories.

The *Improshare* system (12) is focused on an individually oriented reward scheme. The bonus formula takes into consideration the actual hours that an employee has worked. This is compared against a calculated base productivity *value* for this employee. If the base value is greater than the actual hours earned then a bonus is calculated and distributed to employees on a weekly basis.

QWL transitions and legislation throughout the twentieth century.

The quality of work life at the turn of the century is a far cry from what it is today. The extreme of low QWL can be exemplified in 1892 in Homestead, Pennsylvania. It started in 1888 when Coke magnate Henry Clay Frick was hired as general manager of the

58

Carnegie Steel Company after his Coke business was acquired by the Carnegie Steel Company though the purchase of a majority of its stock. Mr. Frick was blatantly and unequivocally against labor unions. In June 1892, when the plants labor contract was about to expire, Mr. Frick decided to institute a wage cut. In anticipation of a strike, he hired 300 armed Pinkerton detectives, as scabs, and barged them up the river behind the plant. This prompted a fierce battle between the Pinkerton *scabs* and the union workers. With the help of a cannon and the use of burning oil on the river, the Pinkertons surrendered. In response to this Mr. Frick gained the support of the governor who in turn used the state militia to take over the plant. Carnegie Steel was then reopened with strike-breakers. Dozens were killed and hundreds were injured as a result of this quality of work life collective bargaining effort. (44)

Although dwarfed by the Carnegie Steel case, many other benefits that we take for granted today were not existent in the early 1900's. There was no *social security*, no *unemployment benefits*, no *workers' compensation*, no assurance of ever realizing earned *pensions*, no government regulation of *health and safety*, and no *anti-discrimination* laws regarding race, color, sex, nationality, religion, or age.

Much in the way of government regulation has been instituted in the 20th century towards improving the quality of work life. The most noteworthy legislation includes: <u>The National Relations Act,</u> (The Wagner Act- 1935), which gave employees the right to engage in union activities; the Fair Labor Standards Act (1938), which established minimum wages, overtime compensation and sexual equality pay standards; the <u>Civil Rights Act</u> (1964); the <u>Equal Employment Opportunity Act</u> (1972); the <u>Age Discrimination in Employment Act</u> (1967). All enacted to enforce the premise that employees must be judged by their abilities and not on the basis of race, color, nationality, sex, religion, or age. The <u>Occupational Safety and Healthy Act</u> (1970), enacted to prove a safe and healthy work environment "free from recognizable hazards"; the Unemployment Compensation Laws enacted to provide minimal income support to the unemployed while seeking new employment; the <u>Norris LaGuardia Act</u> (1932), enacted to assure employee rights to organize and bargain; the <u>Landrum-Griffin Act</u> (1959), which opened the door for the federal government to scrutinize internal operations and financing on union activities.

The natural outgrowth of this preponderance of pro-labor legislation was the creation of the <u>National Labor Relations Board (NLRB)</u>. Originally created from the Wagner Act in 1935 and enhanced by the Taft-Hartley Act in 1947, the NLRB has the responsibility the supervise Union elections and certify successful unions. It also has the jurisdiction to review and judge the outcome of employee or employee initiated charges of unfair labor practices.

Measuring the Quality of Work Life

One of the primary functions of a labor-management (QWL) committee should be to assure that all programs are considered to be dynamic systems that are periodically measured and improved on an ongoing basis.

General indicators of *quality of work life* status include *sick leave usage, accident types and frequency, employee turnover, grievance magnitude and frequency, level of morale, participation in cost savings suggestions and whether or not employees feel the need to collectively organize*. These indicators can be readily obtained from existing records and informal assessments and observations. However, a more informative approach might be to conduct a planned organizational survey. To be effective this survey must be carefully designed with clearly defined assessment objective in mind, data must be obtained from a sample that represents the population being assessed, and it must be collected with time considerations in mind and analyzed using statistically valid techniques. Resultant information must then be clearly presented to the management-labor committee which must subsequently plan for quality of work Life improvement and implement them in a timely manner to enhance employee motivation and assure relevancy.

In addition to humanitarian purposes, quality of work life assessments can show trends that need to be corrected if efforts toward unionization are to be avoided. A study (64, 65) of 87, 740 employees have shown that dissatisfaction with supervisors was the major precursor to union organization activity.

Training

Since all employees in an organization affect the ultimate quality of the system, all should be properly trained so as to understand their jobs and to attain and maintain proficiency in executing them.

An *organizational needs assessment* is the first step in any training program. This is where the trainer will ascertain what the training is meant to accomplish, the relevant *background and capability* of the trainees, and if the needs may be accomplished with *budgetary constraints*.

This phase of training is followed by *curricular development* and *training requirements documentation*.

With this information, the *training champion* can seek *buy-in* from upper management regarding the proposed training.

Post training effectiveness assessments regarding content, delivery, media, meeting times and locations, etc are important preliminary tools to the determining the quality of the training itself.

More important, an assessment of the effects of training *within the relevant functional areas* will help to ascertain overall effectiveness.

63

Quality training can be considered to fit into two general categories, *skills training* and *training in the quality sciences*. Skills training would include such topics as process training for assembly operators, surgical techniques for surgeons, or communications skills training for top management. *Design for manufacturability, design for serviceability* and *testability* courses for engineers and scientists would fit into this category. The primary concern of the quality department regarding skills training is to assure that appropriate foundation skills training is *planned for, completed, verified, documented and upgraded as required*. Skills training is typically coordinated through the Human Resources department and/or through the applicable functional managers.

In a progressive human resources oriented organization, both foundation skills and quality sciences training would be made mandatory via an organized MBO system.

The quality department typically takes a more active role in the development and execution of training in the quality sciences. Often in a total quality revamped organization, a quality education department is chartered with the quality sciences training task.

The quality sciences can be divided into several general categories. The basic category would include topics regarding problem solving techniques, such as *statistical process control, data collection and analysis, and lower level quality policy and procedural development.* Basic quality science skills would typically be made available to all employees in an organization.

Intermediate quality science skills would include both analytical topics, such as basic design of experiments, and financial aspects of *policy deployment* and *quality function deployment.* This level of training would typically be made available to technical and professional employees up to the middle management category. Concise executive awareness sessions are often made available to higher levels of management that have neither the need nor the time for in-depth training in the intermediate quality science skills.

The advanced category of quality sciences training is usually reserved for scientists, engineers, and mathematicians with advanced analytical skills. Advanced topics would include *statistical simulations* of products and processes, reliability sciences and geometric dimensioning and tolerancing.

Aspects of *global quality* approaches, including *Six Sigma,* Lean *Processing and Kaizen systems*, might be positioned throughout many strata of the organization.

Training innovations in the psychosocial and economic domains will be needed to usher in the next generation of *holistic quality oriented organizations*.

Human resources quality courses would include, but not be limited to, such topics as:
- The relationship *between management by objectives systems* and product quality
- Mandatory training and product development plans.
- Quality of work life surveying, interpretation, and interventions.
- Recruiting into and staffing functional departments with quality professionals.
- The quality education MIS tracking system
- Stress leadership
- Time management

The *financial aspects of quality course* would include, but not be limited to the topics regarding:
- The quality of earnings
- Use of confidence intervals and statistical techniques for financial analysis
- Risk indicators
- Cost of quality Accounting
- Quality prioritizations

Quality MIS and Communications Systems

In order to have an effective continuous improvement system, the results of *quality evaluations and analyses* must be *effectively communicated*, in a *timely manner*, to key players in the improvement process.

What needs to be communicated must be determined, along with *how* it is going to be communicated and to *whom* the communications are to be directed. Both manual and automated MIS systems can be used for this purpose.

The quality management information system must be correlated to the functional aspects of the organizations management infrastructure. The mechanisms of data accumulation, analysis and reporting, real time process controls; automated inspection and computer aided scheduling techniques are becoming commonplace in most large quality organizations. The efficient use of these sometimes extravagant systems has become one of the greatest cost concerns of quality management. Cost/benefit analysis is often done after the fact with resulting embarrassment, or worse, for 'cost draining champions'.

Motivating factors must be considered, ideally on an individual basis, but practically on the basis of departmental function. For example accountants and

CEO's are typically *cognitively* motivated by facts and figures, in terms of dollars and cents, whereas Human resources personnel may tend to be *socially* motivated by the humanistic factors of workmanship quality, such as pride and self esteem. (59)

A basic rule of thumb is to focus quality communications and *costs* for all budget accountable management, and on the *applicable* technical concerns for functional employees.

Ideally, operational workers should check their own work and that of previous workers in the work flow process, (when applicable). This system is usually enhanced by, but often replaced by, quality inspectors and auditors working outside of the functional area. *Feedback* should have an immediate verbal element which is backed up by documentation. The 'documentation' would typically be in terms of *handwritten* defect reports or data directly entered into a data base terminal. *Control charting* would be included in this phase of feedback. The *data* obtained is then typically transformed into *information* by a computer program and reviewed by an *analyst* for significant trends over a specified time period.

All MIS systems need to have a function that coordinates; *operations*, such as data input and report distribution; *development* including system design and

68

user training; and *technical support*, including product section and software modification. (23)

Special concerns regarding the quality department include staffing problems and the duplication of the efforts of functional managers outside the quality organization. Quality departments typically have *amateur* MIS professionals within their departments that are often called upon or volunteer to set up and implement systems that end up being very inefficient and sometimes increase quality *appraisal costs* more than they help to decrease product *failure costs*. It is not uncommon to have highly educated engineers spending days on end *hunt and peck* typing quality reports while complex technical problems are being ignored, to *get those reports out on time*. Quality cost analysis is an absolute necessity for such *data intensive* functions as the typical quality department in a large organization. Duplication of efforts can be a special problem because *functional* departments may have similar information needs as the quality department. The importance of inter-departmental communication and participation, initiated at the planning phase of a quality MIS system cannot be over emphasized.

Conflict within Organizations

Factors related to motivation and satisfaction are at the root of much of the loss associated with the human side of quality. *Intrinsic dissonance* occurs when there is a disconnect between our internal drives and the reality of our work situation; while *extrinsic dissonance* might be considered to be a disconnect between our expectations or perceptions of fairness and that which has really manifest in our work situation. Of course, the impact of the external factors are also associated with our internal states, so one could say that extrinsic dissonance is also related to intrinsic dissonance.

Maslow's hierarchy of needs is a very simple way to understand how our internal motivational factors are related to our unique situations. In its simplest form, Maslow's hierarchy can be thought of a as a stairway comprised of ascending steps. Like is a real staircase, the lower step must be passed before the next higher ones are ascended.

The lowest step relates to our *physical needs*, including those concerning food, clothing and housing. Ways of coping with illness may also be considered to fit onto this part of the staircase. If you've even driven a long distance and had to go to the bathroom where there are no bathrooms, you will understand the power of this step. You're not going any further until and nothing else will get done until you relieve yourself.

In the workplace, *the employee who squanders his or her money on drugs, alcohol, cigarettes or gambling may not have enough money to support their basic needs*. On the other hand, the employer who is cheap with salaries, raises and well deserved promotions is in fact hurting both quality and productivity. The employee stuck on this rung if often more interested in finding another job, working at a second one or often being preoccupied with their lack.

The employer who creates an *overtime culture* is foolish to the max when it comes to getting the most out of employees; especially those stuck on step one of the hierarchy. They may be so stressed out by the circumstances in their lives that a much needed hike after work, or a yoga, meditation or nutrition class, would do both employer and employee much better.

I once knew an employee who while he had a decent job had lots of expenses and needed to have other means of income. His boss was an overtime 'enthusiast.' It was interesting that even though the boss came in early and left late, he usually produced much less than other managers who stuck to the normal work schedule. Knowing that the boss stayed late, and was housed in a different building, this employee would come in late, and then sell shoes and trade stocks for most of the day. Another person working in the same department, would hang out and B S in the fitness center till about noon almost every day, then again be commended for staying late as his boss noticed this 'exemplary employee' for staying late, regardless of his low accomplishment level.

Step two in the simplified model is related to security. Once we find that much needed restroom, we are more apt to resume obeying the speed limits and staying in our driving lanes. In our work situations, once we are making an appropriate salary we are more apt to stay at a job that is secure and safe.

On the other hand, if our self-esteem is adequate and we are confident that we have marketable skills, the employee is more apt to leave a job that they think is in an unsafe area. For example, many successful employees left Manhattan to seek employment elsewhere after the 911 terrorist attacks on the world trade center. Those less confident about their job skills were more apt to stay.

After step three in the hierarchy is ascended, and the employee is well fed and has an adequate wardrobe to get started, the social drives of step three are apt to kick in.

As social beings, most employees find that their relationships at work are at least as important as what they do on the job. This is such an important factor that those that we tend to hang out with at work are considered to be our primary work group, while our formal relationship with our boss and other work associates is considered to be the secondary group in the organizational and industrial psychology literature.

In order to fulfill this intrinsic need, the astute employer will take several steps, some even unofficially, to create a productive high quality workgroup. While the *structured interview* and employment form may provide useful information about how new recruits might interact, *biodata* about new is often found out in other ways.

Referrals from *existing employees* are not only the most useful types, as no one wants to look bad for referring a lousy employee, but they may also lead to informal information about the potential employee. Information about their hobbies, what school they attended, the religious, moral and political views tell lots about how they might interact with others at work. Even the lunch interview is commonly used to get to better know potential employees.

If you have a department of rock climbers, and use bring in an Asian superstar whose sole hobby is working harder after the work days ends, or only playing chess and videogames, the lack of fit might far outweigh any potential gains from intellectual competence.

In another case that readily comes to mind, an employee would chit chat on the phone for most of the day, helping to fulfill her need for social interaction. Since she realized that she had an in with the boss, she had little fear she would get fired for goofing off several hours per day. This protection allowed her to not worry about the physical needs or loosing the security of having a nice office space in a safe building within a safe corporate setting.

Since the boss favored her among other employees, her self-esteem was also enhanced. Accordingly, she had made to step four of the hierarchy of needs.

Unfortunately, other employees had noticed the favoritism and thought it was unfair to them and other hard working, dedicated employees. The inequity had started a flurry of bad feelings within the department as this extrinsic de motivator was allowed to continue for several years unchecked.

The favored employee did go on to reach the highest level of the hierarchy, step five, self-actualization, as she continued her career outside of the company.

At the same company, a young gentleman was not given the promotion that he had expected. During a

74

time of financial struggles, the promotions had become limited and therefore more competitive in nature. When the boss gave the scarce commodity, the promotion, to her friend instead, the young man was livid to say the least.

This very fit and very dedicated employee suffered a stroke that very evening, while participating in a regular sporting activity. The combined stress of not reaching his career goals, not only hurt his self-esteem and chances of reaching *self-actualization*, his thwarted expectation of a promotion was also made worse by the inequity of another person not getting the job that he was expecting to get.

Since the typical manager may spend up to 25 percent of their time in conflict management, the cost of HR Quality associated may be associated with:

1) Not understanding the intrinsic motivators of key employees

2) Not honoring the expectations of same

3) And, not being equitable

Cost the company a bundle of obvious costs. However, this was just the tip of the iceberg, as many other employees became not only disgruntled, but the associated gossip and other ramifications were very expensive indeed.

Financial Aspects of Holistic Quality Systems

In modern societies, organizational gain is typically measured by financial profitability, while behavioral considerations usually take a less than primary role. This is true in all industrialized countries, including those in the Americas, Africa and Asia. The European *Economic Community* certainly portrays financial concepts by virtue of its very name.

Ironically, the very quality systems used to measure profitability may need to be carefully scrutinized, in terms of both accounting and statistical validity, in typical organizations. The purpose of this section is to shed light on *financial quality system* indicators and some potentially viable ways to continuously improve them.

Quality of Earnings

An often neglected aspect of an organizational quality system is the utilization of quality criteria to assess the nature of an enterprise's earnings (15). Included in this type analysis would be criteria used to judge:
- The *risk* associated with stockholders equity and debt.

- The *variability* and *stability* of key financial parameters and ratios.
- *Consistency*, *conservancy* and statistical validity of accounting policy.
- The *predictability* of future earnings.
- The *clarity*, *relevance* and *appropriateness* of the financial reporting system.

The sensitivity of an enterprises' securities to fluctuations in the market, called the <u>beta</u> factor, would be an external measurement factor indicative of the degree of risk associated with investing in the enterprise. (Note however that risk of this nature tends to be inversely proportional to reward.)

The degree of *leverage* used in the capitol structure of a company would be an internal factor used to measure risk. The *debt to equity*, *debt to total assets* and *debt to capitalization ratios* are common quality indicators used for this purpose.

The *variability* of key financial indictors from expected trend lines is one indicator that can be used to measure the validity of organizational plans contingent upon these indicators. Prediction of future performance would be proportional to the variability of past and present performance. The usefulness of analytical techniques such as sensitively and scenario analyses would also be related to an alternative to the use of interval estimation is the use of a standard tolerance (such as +/- 10%) to be assigned to financial parameters. Analysis such as a net present value calculation could then be calculated using incremental cash flows assumed to be at each tolerance *extreme*.

For example, if a project cost $4169 and it was expected that revenues of $1000 for the present year and the following four years could be realized, then if revenue was calculated at the $1000 nominal value the project would have a breakeven NPV of 0 (based on a 10% rate of return). At the lower 10% tolerance limit the NPV would be -$450 (with the project possibly being rejected). At the upper tolerance limit the NPV would be $417. Note that a spread of $867 was calculated based on the same data subject to a 10% tolerance shift!

The quality of predictions based on a confidence or tolerance interval is clearly superior to that which is based on a single point estimate. *Clarity, relevance*, and *appropriateness* of the financial reporting system can be evaluated by questioning and comparing the intentions of the financial report *suppliers* versus what the customer functions thought was communicated, what was expected, and what was needed.

Cost of Quality Accounting Systems

Cost of quality accounting systems are <u>managerial</u> accounting systems initiated during the 1950's to facilitate communication with management using the common media of dollars and cents. The benefits of using this type of accounting would include; the identification of problem areas, the provision of a standard measurement basis, and having a framework to help in the budgeting allocation process.

Among the primary factors required to reduce costs is an understanding of what they are, where they come from, how they can be categorized and what influences are constraining them.

By creative logic it can be implied that virtually all costs in excess of the minimum required for production can be considered to be quality costs. Obviously the rules of sensible prioritization must be applied. Some general characteristics of quality costs are that they're *avoidable*, that they would be nonexistent if there were no *nonconformities* and that they needed to assure *fitness for use*. The priority list of costs to be tracked typically comes from accounting data and estimations from quality professionals. (22)

Categorization is often used as a method to better understand cause and affect relationships and to obtain guidance in terms of optimizing the impact of spending, focused on minimizing quality costs. Traditional quality cost categories include internal failure costs, external failure costs, appraised costs and prevention costs. The costs of *prevention* (i.e. quality planning and training) and *appraisal* (i.e. auditing and testing) have a nonlinear inverse relationship with the costs of internal (i.e. scrap and rework) and external (i.e. customer service and recalls) failures. Choosing the *feasible region* of balance between these opposing factions takes considerable managerial judgment and forecasting capability. Optimization could be facilitated by the use of such operations research techniques as linear programming and simulation, although I'm not ware of any related studies or applications. The primary objective is (or should be) to maximize profits by minimizing *total* costs. Sometimes the perfectionist tendencies of these *craftsmen* (28) and the power plays of the quality jungle fighter have to be compromised in order to remain productive and not be trapped by the desire to be impractically perfectionist. Typically when; no more profitable failure reduction projects are viable; appropriate appraisal methods and standards have been verified, and prevention projects have been transferred to improvement projects, then quality costs can be considered to have approached optimization.

Ratio analysis (4) can be readily adapted to (COQ) accounting systems. For example COQ vs. cost of units shipped, net revenue, cost of labor and costs of total overhead can be appropriately included in a (COQ) tracking and reporting system.

Planning and implementation of COQ system requires provisions for both diligence and diplomacy. Definition of collection and tabulation mechanisms and report analyses and distribution must remain consistent, accurate and management oriented to assure that *communications transactions* are effective. (28).

The management of the departments or cost centers being reported on may become very defensive if they feel that their gamesmanship* interest has been compromised during COQ disclosures. Therefore it is very important to practice participative management during both the planning and control phases of the project if cooperation and <u>buy-in</u> is expected and *retaliation* is to be avoided (This includes neck injuries from have to watch your back so often)

---

*gamesmen are highly competitive individuals and team players. Although they usually believe that their goals are merged with company goals (28), differences of opinion can cause severe animosity to develop. Especially when basic motivational hierarchal needs are being threatened (42). (Such as loss of money and/or a job.)

82

Quantitative Aspects of Holistic Quality Systems

The concept of continuous improvement can be quite vague and nebulous without concrete standards of measurement and comparison. The quantitative aspects of quality systems add the dimension of tangibility to the *service* characteristics of MBO objectives, behavioral impact studies, and financial and engineering quality indicator analysis. The sense of credibility and reality is certainly enhanced by the judicious use of statistics when evaluating traditionally mathematically oriented functions, such as those in the areas of the natural and behavioral sciences, engineering and finance.

Quantitative Techniques

Integrated organizational quality systems could be considered to be analogous to the human nervous system with both qualitative and quantitative functional aspects, like the hemispheres of the brain. The analytical functions of the left side of the brain must be balanced by the aspects of the right side of the brain to be effective. The Japanese would consider this to be the *yang (masculine)* and *yin (feminine)* aspects of a system.

The quantitative aspects of a quality system are used to objectively measure performance and to have valid and repeatable criteria for comparison. Applicable and appropriate techniques can be applied to most aspects of an organization including such divergent concepts as the efficiency of janitors and the psychological impact of the words used in a mission statement.

The purpose of this section is to briefly describe several basic quantitative techniques that are applicable to organizational quality systems, and to suggest several (often uncommon) possibilities for their use.

The initial steps in any quantitative analysis is to plan how to collect raw data, how to analysis it and how to effectively communicate the resulting information.

Statistical Techniques

The *pareato principle* is one of the most commonly applicable quantitative rules. The most basic tenant of *pareato analysis* is that in most systems there are the *vital few* and the *trivial many* aspects regarding impact. It is commonly stated that most often roughly 20% of systems members contribute to roughly 80% of factory costs. This phenomenon is typically called the 80/20 rule. Vilfredo Pareto, an Italian economist (1848-1923), and M.O. Loren, an American

84

statistician, have found these principles to be prevalent in describing economic distributions. (22)

A *pareato defect analysis* simply involves counting the number of defects and assigning percentages to each known contributor. Corrective action can be focused on the *vital few* contributors in a priority fashion. The most common way to display the result is to use a bar graph or a pie graph.

A *histogram* is a specialized bar graph most commonly used to describe the frequency of occurrence within a grouping of continuous intervals. The intervals are evenly spaced and typically chosen for clarity and relevance to the variables being analyzed. The tallying method used to describe the number of occurrences in each interval is called the *frequency distribution* among adjacent intervals. Histograms can be quite useful to describe electronic, mechanical and chemical interval measurements. Human resource quality indicators, such as weight and cholesterol relationships to cardiovascular problems and efficiency vs. time on a job are readily amenable to histogram displaying techniques.

Frequency distributions typically have a characteristic shape which describes the way observations accumulate within and are dispersed among intervals. These shapes can often be described as measures of *central tendency and dispersion*. The arithmetic mean, or ordinary average; the median, which is the value of which half the values of the population exceed and half do not; and the mode, the value which occurs most often in the data; are measures of central tendency. Measures of dispersion include the range, which is the difference between the minimum and maximum values in data; and the standard deviation, which is a measure of the sum of the variation between the arithmetic mean and each of the data variables. The smaller the standard deviation the closer the variables are to the average.

A *probability distribution* function is a mathematical formula which relates to the values of a characteristic with their probability of occurrence in a population from which a randomly chosen representative sample has been analyzed. When the characteristic can take on any value, (to a specified degree of accuracy) the probability distribution is one restricted to whole-number or integer values. Among the most widely used discrete contribution are the *normal* and the *exponential* distribution. The most commonly used discrete distributions are the *poison* and the *binomial.*

The normal distribution is applicable when the values are focused about the arithmetic mean with an equal chance of being above or below it. The T distribution is an approximation to the normal distribution typically used for samples with less than 30 members.

The exponential distribution is applicable when more observations are likely to occur below the average than above it. It is often used to describe the interval of time or space to get the *first success,* such as the time it takes for the first customer to enter a store or fan an electronic capacitor to discharge its voltage to a certain value. (22)

Both the binomial and the Poisson distributions are applicable for estimating the probability of occurrences of an event out of a specified number of trails; with a known probability of occurrence on teach trial. (The Poisson distribution is used when the probability is less than 10% on each trail and the sample size is at least 16). Typical uses for these distributions are the number of returns from a department store or the number of defectives expected in a lot of components. There are various statistical tests that can be used to help 'fit' data to the most appropriate distribution. One such test is the Kolmogorov-Smirnov test. (10)

Scatter diagrams are used to graphically portray the relationship between dependent and independent variables. While *linear regression* is an analytical technique used to fit the most appropriate 'line' through the scatter plot when the relationship is linear. The resulting regression line equation can be used to estimate expected values of a dependant variable given an independent one. (Note that this technique is valid only in the region where the original data is taken.)

Extrapolation can lead to gross errors. The quality applications for regression analysis are quite numerous. Included is the relationship between household income and consumption, specific food served in a cafeteria and after lunch productivity, product defects and customer satisfaction, ad infinitem.

Confidence Interval Estimation

This is among the most often neglected, but most useful statistical techniques applicable to a *total quality system.* It's much more typical to see statements such as *the sample mean absenteeism rate last year was 5 days per employee throughout the company rather than using statements such as the sample indicator with 80% confidence, that the mean company absenteeism rate per employee last year was contained in the interval from 2 to 8 days.* In the first statement the use of a simple average is called a point estimate. The second statement was based on a Confidence Interval estimate.

The technique used to determine *confidence interval estimates* are related to the applicable distribution, the sample size, and the acceptable level of risk involved in making the estimate. The implications can be of such a high magnitude that a go/no decision to accept or reject an entire project can be erroneously made based on the improper use of point estimates. Application in the field of financial statement analysis, psychological evaluations, engineering tolerancing and market surveying would surely be enhanced by the use of this technique. Note that the accuracy of a market survey based on a sample size of 100 would be accurate within +/- 9.8% of the population parameter versus an accuracy of +/- 2.5% if a sample size of 1500 is used (at the 95% confidence level). The latter survey is nearly four times as accurate. (18)

Control Charts

During the 1920's, the control chart was developed by Dr. Walter A. Shewhart while he worked at Bell Laboratories. The primary tenant behind this significant U.S. contribution to quality sciences is that the quality of virtually any parameter is subject to a certain amount of random chance. Over time a stable system of random fluctuation will develop which is inherent in the process. Reasons for variation from this stable pattern can be detected and corrected if the limits of the pattern are known. This is the purpose of a control chart. (13)

A control chart is essentially a graphic portrayal of a probability distribution turned on its side. Horizontal lines are typically drawn on the chart which represent the process arithmetic <u>mean</u> and the upper and lower <u>control limits</u> (which hare typically equal to +/- two or three standard deviations from the mean.)

Control charts can be created for both variable (continuous) and attributes (discreet) date. Common types of control charts are *average and range, average and standard deviation, fraction rejected number on non-conformances per unit* and *total nonconformance per total units inspected.* The manufacturing uses are obvious.

Some less obvious applications versus time might include; *the advertising to sales ratio, absenteeism rates,* the *ratio of engineering changes completed versus those in queue, number of employees trained,* select financial statement ratios, *number of on time deliveries versus the number of lots purchased, average number of miles walked* during a fitness orientated organizational development intervention, etc.

Analysis of Variance, F Tests, Chi Square techniques and hypothesis testing are among the statistical techniques typically used to determine if there is a significant difference between parameters being compared. Sample sizes and level of acceptable risk* are considered in each of these techniques. It's extremely important to realize that without taking these factors into consideration the *quality of data comparisons* could be seriously low or even purposefully misleading.

For example, an average trend of net sales to net profiles ratios for a three month period may not be appropriately compared (for variability) to a similar ratio for a 36 month period without taking sample size, standard deviation and significance testing into consideration. Such economically significant practices as financial statement analysis may be invalid, in my opinion, without taking these factors into consideration when they're applicable.

*risk= 1-confidence level

Product Reliability and Maintainability

Product reliability and maintainability regards the probability that a functional characteristic will perform a required function, under stated conditions for a stated period of time or specified number of cycles or events.

At the early design phase, *predictions* are made regarding the probability of failure in terms of mean time to failure, between failures, before or between service calls, before or between maintenance or repair actions, and the like. Predictions are based on historical results experienced with similar components, products or systems. This information is typically found in military hand books and in *in house* records. A thorough analysis would include a description of the most likely failure modes (types) to be experienced under given environmental conditions, along with the relative criticality of each anticipated failure type. This process is called *failure mode effects and criticality analysis* (FMECA.)

Subsequent to making predictions, the reliability representative often makes recommendations to improve the reliability of the initial designs. Typical recommendations would include the use of *redundant* components of subsystems and the use of a back up motor that switches on when the primary one fails. *Derating* involves using components that are nominally rated for usage beyond the respective application. The use of an official fire hose to water the garden, under normal residential water pressure, would be an example of *derating*. Sound economic analysis and judgment must be used to evaluate the viability of these tradeoffs.

The reliability department also coordinates the *simulated life testing* of products. This involves the use of environmental extremes, such as temperature, humidity or pressure cycling used to simulate specified product lives. <u>Actual usage</u> testing, such as customer field testing (and tracking) is typically coordinated by the reliability department in collaboration with the marketing department.

During the manufacturing product phase, the reliability department often leads the *failure analysis group*. This team is chartered to analyze and recommend corrective actions regarding non-trivial failures.

One of the most esoteric of the reliability sub sciences is the *human factors engineering* function. The primary focus of this function is to assess the physiological and psychological impact of products. Often called ergonomics, this fascinating science is used to evaluate *aesthetic* criteria including color, texture, weight, orientation of indicator dials and lamps, seating comfort, lighting, sound, knob turning resistance, etc.

The reliability function typically coordinates the development of product warrantees. Reliability engineering assistance is often sought during product liability investigations in conjunction with the legal and safety departments.

It's quite evident that the often neglected sub science of reliability can be an important portal to the customers of a total quality oriented organization.

Management Science/Operations Research

An often neglected, but potentially powerful, set of tools for strategic quality planning and renewal are those from the realm of the management sciences. *Simulation*, *optimization* and *decision analysis* are among the potentially most effective tools for this purpose. Assurance that these and related techniques are included in the quality plans of the next generation of total quality oriented organizations.

Simulation is basically a technique whereby a mathematical model is developed (based on past trends and inherent mathematical relationships) to describe a system and to predict how that system will respond to a set of changing conditions at a specified level of certainty. The variables in the model are typically varied in a random fashion to simulate natural occurrences. From the range of the results of simulations, realistic quality goals can be determined, on the *range* of the results of the simulations.

94

For example, before yield improving goals are set for a stable process, it's important to know the likely range of the expected yield under normal conditions. This is analogous to the confidence interval concept discussed earlier. (I've prepared an example which is disclosed in the exhibit section.) *Monte Carlo Simulation* techniques were used for this purpose.

Scenario analyses (45) can be used, as one method to describe potential econometric changes in a national market. *Sensitivity analysis* (45) can be used to ascertain the stability of indicators, such as elasticity of supply or demand, under changing conditions. From this type of information, analytically sound quality goals and indicators can be developed inclusive of marketing, finance, purchasing and other *service* functions.

Optimization techniques such as *linear and non linear programming* (39) can be used to ascertain the most appropriate set of solutions, called the feasible region, and the optimum solution, given that a series of constraints (boundaries) are imposed. In the area of preventative quality assurance, the benefits can be very high. For example, equations can be utilized to determine the ideal combination of process inspectors vs. operators that would be expected to minimize quality costs while maiming output.

Among the most popular decision analyses techniques used by quality professions, is the *Ishikawa cause and effect diagram* (see exhibit MS1). Developed in 1950 by Professor Kaoru Ishikawa, of Tokyo University, the Japanese also use the name Tokusei Yoin Zu (Characteristic diagram) and Sakana No Hone (fishbone) diagram. (22) The effect or problem under investigation is assigned to the *fish's* spinal column. Primary potential contributors can be considered to be ribs, and so on. The finalized diagram provides a visual road for further investigations of both a quantitative and qualitative nature.

The qualitative aspects of the loss function can be extended to consider variation losses as contributing to scrap, rework and recalls (due to preference for "on target" parameters and the probability of a quicker degradation to *out of spec* conditions for parameters initially farther away from the ideal specified condition. The Japanese consider the economic and cultural implications as extending throughout society. Some western quality *philosophers* are starting to think likewise, more taoistically.

Calculation of Confidence Interval Estimates

Since many of the variables used in business analyses are *normally or near normally distributed*, and the population standard deviation is seldom known, the t distribution is often utilized. For the t-distribution the confidence interval used for the <u>mean</u> of the date would be:

X bar – S x bar x t (n-1) 2/2 <= M =< X bar + S xbar x t(n-1) 2/2

Where:
- X equals the sample average
- S x equals the sample standard deviations divided by the square root of the sample size
- N equals the sample size
- 2 equals 1-the confidence level

t n-1 2/2 is the table statistic value used to represent the t value that bounds tail of a standard t distribution with the tail area equal to (1- the confidence)/ 2 with n-1 degrees of freedom (see standard t table.)

Simulation

Method:
Average process yield is currently calculated by subtracting the average decimal percent defective from one, for each manufacturing code, and sequentially multiplying this times the same calculation for each code, i.e.: (1-.05) (1-.06) (10.01) …. While this method does have validity, it can be a very misleading representation of what can be

expected on a real world day to day basis under expected conditions of random variation.

This scenario has been simulated by considering that the random distribution of each code can be represented by a Poisson distribution which is distributed about the empirically measured average percent defective. Using a cumulative Poisson distribution table, I assigned numbers to represent each cumulative probability class, for each distribution, based on average percent defective. For example, for the average defect category of one percent, I assigned zero defects to numbers between 000 and 367 representing 368/ 1000 of the population and three defects to the group 920 and 980. The simulation was next performed by choosing random numbers, from a random number table, representing each manufacturing code and calculating the process yield for each 'run' of the simulation.

Results:
The results of six process yield simulations have had yields ranging from 49 to 62 percent. This was based on Poisson distributions distributed around average code yields where total calculated process yield was 58 percent.

Conclusions:

A change from 49 to 62 percent represents a 13 percent difference in process yield or an increase of 26 percent, if based on a change from 44 percent. Note that more simulations or a consideration of + - 3 sigma approximations would yield an even greater variation, <u>without shifting the base process</u> averages! It can be concluded that periodic fluctuations of 10 to 15 percent in this particular calculated process yield might not be reason for panic or elation (as considered presently). This magnitude of change may just represent random variations in a reasonable stable process. The results of this very enlightening exercise may very well lead to more appropriate process performance indicators to be used in my business unit.

For example, an indicator that combines average process yield with the variance of the processes might lead to a more realistic measurement yardstick. This model could be expanded, computerized and used to simulate the *real world* effects of projected process changes.

In this realistic simulation example, a real manufacturing process yield was simulated using *Monte Carlo simulation* based upon a *Poisson distribution* and *confidence level interval estimates*.

To make the illustration easy to follow, let us assume that the process yield goal was 95 percent and that the 80 percent confidence level range - BASED UPON EXPECTED VARIATION – was approximately 91 – 99 percent.

So then, when the process dips below 95 percent, there was **really nothing to worry about**. On the other hand, if the process is between 95 and 99 percent, there is **nothing to be elated about either**. In the world of statistics, anything in the range of 91-99 percent is **considered to be one and the same number**.

This point is critically important and may be readily applied to any manufacturing, medical, educational or financial process – for starters.

For all intents and purposes, one angioplasty gone wrong out of a hundred is the same thing as nine gone wrong; or in the world of variation, one banking transaction gone wrong, with a different expected process yield, out of 10,000 transactions, might be the same thing as 15 discrepancies in customer banking statements.

Control Systems

The most traditional form of quality science and technology is that of control. The purpose of quality control is to evaluate the *conformance* of goods and services to *customer* (internal and external) expectations, such as functionality, safety, adequacy, dependability, economy and delivery. Primary elements of control involve; developing qualitative and quantitative *indicators* for evaluation; the execution of evaluation techniques; the mechanisms of feedback; corrective action with verification; and the restructuring of goals to facilitate continuous improvement. The *organizational*, *behavioral*, *quantitative*, and *financial* considerations, discussed thus far, must be carefully adhered to assure effective control.

Online quality control refers to activities including, and relating to, audit and inspection, which is the topic of this section.

Offline quality activities include the preventative techniques, such as *design review*, including failure mode analysis, experimental design, and quality function deployment. Offline quality mechanisms will be discussed in the section regarding new product development quality.

Auditing and Inspection

Organizational <u>control processes</u> are developed to determine how well the results of organizational strategies and objectives conform to their proposed intentions. <u>Control systems</u> must be carefully designed to provide an *optimum amount of information (7) given the constraints of cost, time and benefits derived.* The primary benefits can be defined in terms of a decrease in *internal* and *external* failure costs (22) while the primary costs can be defined in terms of *appraisal* costs and the opportunity costs of time. The trend and the goal are to minimize auditing in proportion to the emphasis towards *designing* quality and reliability into products and processes.

According to ANSI stands N45.2.23 auditing is defined as "a documented activity performed in accordance with written procedures or checklists to verify, by examination and evaluation of objective evidence, that applicable elements have been developed, documented and effectively implemented in accordance with specified requirements. An audit shall not be confused with surveillance or inspection for the sole purpose of process control or product acceptance." There are shades of gray between auditing and inspection. However the difference can be defined by considering that auditing attempts to evaluate the effectiveness of a quality assurance system, while inspection is focused towards the isolated quality of a product or service. Inspection procedures are often part of the auditing process.

One of the primary rules of *statistical process control* is the *rule of 10.* This rule indicates that inspections that find problems at each previous phase of a process are about ten times less costly than if they were fund at the present phase. I'm not sure if the quantitative aspect of this rule has been verified, but the concept is very real. It's obvious that defective components found at incoming receiving inspection are substantially more beneficial than finding them on an assembly line. Finding them at the assembly line is better than finding them at a customer site. Ideally the problem should be *prevented* at the component supplier level.

Auditing can be differentiated into two broad categories, *internal auditing* and *external auditing*. Internal auditing is applied to programs, systems, products and process under the umbrella of the organizations direct control and within its organizational structure. External auditing is applied outside the organization; for example, to suppliers.

Programs and systems, at all organizational levels, are audited for presence, implementation and effectiveness of an integrated quality program, comprehensive enough to be appropriate to the nature of the criteria for the evaluation of; conformance to corporate and regulatory policy, leadership skills of management, planning processes, data management and analysis, human resource utilization, QA/QC and reliability evaluations, internal and external customer satisfaction, quality of earnings, and robustness and optimization of system and product designs to extreme conditions.

Product auditing is most often a reinspection by *quality assurance auditors*, of products of product components from lots previously inspected, by *quality control inspectors*. The purpose of this type of auditing is to evaluate the effectiveness of the Q.C., manufacturing, purchasing, design engineering, test functions, etc. To minimize the costs of redundant inspections, smaller samples are usually audited than were originally inspected. Additionally, a select amount of inspection material is typically chosen at random from the list of total inspection criteria, *critical defects* are usually designated as causing nonfunctionality or safety issues; *major defects* are less severe functionally or those of a significant aesthetic nature; *minor defects* are of a trivial nature either functionally or aesthetically.

Process quality includes, but is not limited to, evaluations of the product audit/inspection system, the integrity of manufacturing documentation, the integrity and calibration test and assembly equipment, housekeeping and safety factors.

Standard *sampling plans* are typically used to help inspection/audit functions choose sample sizes and the number of acceptable rejects, give the lot size and the acceptable quality level (AQL).* The producers risk (probability that a bad lot is accepted) is also specified. (13) Military Standard 105D is the most common set of sampling plans used to evaluate attribute (pass/fail) criteria, while Military Standard 414 is often used for variable criteria.

The psychological aspects of auditing must be carefully considered to assure the effectiveness of the audit program. Good *participative management* techniques (42) should be employed during the planning stage of the program to assure buy-in of the *auditee* functions and to clearly communicate the expected mutual benefits (28) to be expected from the program. During implementation of the audits, auditee management should be invited to accompany the auditors. The decision to forewarn them must also be considered.

Feedback from audits must be clear, concise, of a non-derogatory nature, and presented in a timely nature, to maximize effectiveness.

---

* AQL is usually defined as the worst case quality level, in percentage or ratio, that is still considered acceptable.

Follow-up audits should be conducted to assess corrective action and to reinforce the seriousness of intent.

Select Special Audits

In the organizations of the future, perhaps in a *eupsychian solacracy,** I would expect that comprehensive audits of communications processes, strategic plans, and marketing functions would become commonplace activities. Even the National Award surveys barely touch upon these topics today.

Communications auditing (28) is focused upon both qualitative and quantitative aspects of communications. The usefulness, clarity, motivation strategy behind (i.e. Win-Lose, Win-Win, esteem enhancing, etc.) communications media used, and delivery system (i.e. oral presentation or video) would be included among the qualitative quality indicators.

Quantitative indicators would include the number and length of meetings required to solve a problem, the

---

*A eupsychian solacracy is an organization that is intentional rather than reactive and focused to the maximization of both psychological health and profits.

number of graphs required to portray an issue, and the number of hours engineers and accountants spend per week doing word processing.

Audits of high level organizational strategies (7) can be used to evaluate the effectiveness of the Board of Directors and the top strata of management. Relevant quality indicators for this level of auditing would include, but not be limited to:

- The validity of the reasons for growth of diversification.
- The effectiveness of predicting econometric trends.
- The effectiveness of top/down policy deployment.
- Statistical trends regarding returns on shareholders equity and the effectiveness of dividend policies.
- Psychological impact regarding the wording of mission and policy statements.
- The general health and happiness of the employees!

The set of quality indicators within the domain of marketing functions auditing (24) would relate to; Macro market forecasting capabilities, the fit between market strategies and general corporate strategies, the effectiveness of market planning, analysis and control systems, the returns from marketing expenditures, and profitability of marketing functions including pricing, distribution and advertising activities.

I predict that the next generation of quality audit functions will be staffed primarily by a hybrid group of auditors trained in the traditional statistical/engineering quality sciences and those trained with accounting skills in the areas of business record analyses, financial statement analysis and tax auditing. Since the 1950's, the charter of the Institute of Internal Auditor has overlapped into organizational and policy areas beyond the purely financial while ASQ certified engineers and auditors are becoming more involved in financial areas. Symbiotic organizational groups, where the twain meets, might make sense functionally.

Service Quality Special Considerations

The primary differences between goods and services is that pure goods are completely *tangible* while pure services are *intangible*. Most products contain aspects of both goods and services and are classified according to which aspects predominate.

Quality considerations for service industries are rapidly becoming as important to management as product quality has become during this century. With increasing competition, both domestic and international, it's become a matter of survival to

108

assure that the image of the organization is perceived to be *caring, efficient*, and *aesthetically pleasing*. The cleanliness of Disney World, the quick service at McDonalds, and the caring approach of Digital Equipment Company have unmistakably added profits to these organizations. (21)

Special quality indicators for service organization include; "add-on value factors", such as Sunday banking hours and good looking flight attendants; a balance of *High Touch with High Tech*, such as providing special training on bedside manner for emergency room physicians and painting jail cells with soothing colors; Customized Service Delivery (this can enhance dependence on the uniqueness of the providing organization as well as facilitating psychological bonding by allowing customers to *participate* in service design; and providing *one stop service*, such as "one stop banking" and commuter training courses.

To assure that high integrity service mechanisms are installed, *accountability* must be enhanced at the lowest levels where customer contact is made to assure quick *queuing* and *action* times and a customer perception of 'knowledgability'. *Feedback* channels must be *expedient, accurate*, and *courteous*. Technology can be used to assure the *whole jobs* are completed at the point of contact. A good example is the use of inter library loan access terminals.

Table of Select Quality Indicators

Function	Indicator
Human Resources	- QWL survey results - Absenteeism Rates - Employee turnover - Number of grievances - Percent smokers vs. non smokers
Customer Service & Billing	- Average number of rings before phone is answered - Time to complete standard repairs - Number of billing errors - Delay time from service to billing
Marketing	- Cost of advertising as a % of sales - Percent of actual vs. forecasted sales - Number of customer complaints about pricing - Number of customer Related engineering changes

R &D
- Number of feasible vs. unfeasible concepts per unit time.

Design Engineering
- Number of design changes during engineering & manufacturing phases
- Percentage of changes completed vs. those in queue
- "Design for" scores assembly, Testability, serviceability

Purchasing
- Percentage of on time vs. late deliveries
- Ratio of qualified venders to unqualified venders, per unit time

Airlines
- Number of late flight take offs
- Seat comfort
- Food quality
- Politeness of stewardesses

Telephone Company
- Number of poor connections
- Key cap appearance
- Voice clarity

Medicine
- Number of caesarian births per physician.
- Queuing time in emergency rooms
- Number of 'ghost' surgeries per physician.
- Number of wrong drugs administered.
- Inappropriate conduct
- Number of law suits
- Deaths per hospital stay

Secretarial
- Number of typo's per page
- Time to answer phone

Executives
- Clarity of mission statement
- Relationship between strategic plan and loss
- Management turnover

New Product/Service Development Quality

Holistic quality system planning would ideally be initiated as early as possible in the new product development cycle. Heavy emphasis could rightfully be placed on the synergistic creation of functional new product development plans by both functional groups and the *new product quality section* of the organizations quality structure.

The purpose of this section is to summarize key quality factors in the new product development process, major advances in design and customer integration by the Japanese, and to propose a synopsis of relevant functions for a new product quality section.

Key Quality Factors In the New Product Development Process

The new product development process needs to be systematized into sequential phases with a relatively formalized phase gate approval process. One of the primary elements of a holistic quality system would be for the quality department to participate in the development of this process and to assure that it is carefully documented.

The first phase in the process is typically a joint endeavor between the marketing research department and the strategic product planning group. The goal at this point is research culminating in the creation of formalized, yet flexible, market and customer requirements documentation. Market and customer needs are assessed with consideration of *functional requirements* needed to fulfill them, the time frame that they're perceived to persist and the general *value* range that they would be willing to pay to realize their desires. The competitive environment is evaluated for potential threats, by a *vectorial approach*, which would be in terms of magnitude, direction and starting position. Finally the initial correlation between these factors and strategic plans would be documented.

Approval to enter the concept and feasibility study phases of a proposed project is typically contingent upon upper management approval of the initial proposal. This package would include the Market Requirements Document along with feasibility study plans and associated funding requirements.

The *feasibility study* phase would consist of product *concept* and *obsolescence* studies conducted by marketing; technological requirements and *capability* studies conducted by Research and Development; scheduling estimations and facilities planning conducted by the programs planning department and advanced manufacturing engineering; and initial <u>cost</u> *estimations* conducted by the finance, design engineering, and advanced manufacturing engineering departments.

If the prospective project is considered feasible then a comprehensive *program plan* is developed and formalized to provide an integrated structure for the project. Milestones, commitments and formalization of documentation requirements are more strictly enforced after this transition point between the potential project stigma and *full steam ahead* designation. The financial objectives are planned for including required returns on investment with associated cash flows.

These are transposed into *marketing and sales goals* with their associated plans. They must include market forecasts, distribution plans, pricing strategies, promotional plans; sales force training and equipment plans, and plans to develop the product specification jointly with design engineering.

Design engineering's sub plan must provide for the development of engineering models and prototypes. This would include joint component selection and *qualification* plans with the new product purchasing and quality departments as well as model and prototype qualification test plans developed jointly with the product reliability and quality departments.

Manufacturing departments are commonly starting to work simultaneously with design engineering to assure that manufacturing equipment, manpower and quality plans are started at the proper time to allow for program lags. There's also a present focus to assure that new products are *assembleable, testable* and *serviceable.*

Marketing and sales requirements include supplements containing approval of the advertising and promotional program; the availability of demonstration equipment; and the verification of a forecasting system, with an approved product specific forecast.

The service plan elements would include: the approval of a service plan; the completion of service and customer manuals; the installation of a customer assistance center and the inclusion of new product criteria in the post manufacturing product tracking (MIS) system.

The final phase in the process is the approval of ship acceptance documentation. The purpose of this documentation is to assure that all elements of the program have been satisfactorily completed to permit unlimited product launch and final release to mass markets.

Designing High Quality Products

During the 1970's the emphasis of Japanese Quality Systems was moving away from *on line,* after the fact approaches, towards designing quality into products. The most prominent Japanese proponent of this approach is Dr. Genichi Taguchi. Dr. Taguchi's approach is a synthesis of both philosophy and engineering design. (38)

Dr. Taguchi maintains that quality is a measure of the loss imparted to society by a product. The loss is considered to be a function of the deviation of specifications from target values. For example, a transmission made with gears manufactured at the specification limits would tend to be noisier than one whose components were made at the nominal target value. Deterioration to failure would be faster and would hence impart losses to the consumer, the company, and to society in general.

In order to maximize conformance to specifications and *minimize variability*, *designed experiments* are performed on products and processes. The experiments are designed in such a way that many factors are varied simultaneously. The results observed are next analyzed in such a way that the optimal combination of levels of factors is discerned. This type of experimentation can save an enormous amount of time. For example, if 2 levels of 7 variables were varied at one time, it would take 128 experiments to test all combinations. The same information can be obtained from seven experimental runs if it is designed properly.

The uniqueness of the Taguchi approach comes from the fact that while various combinations of factors are being configured, each configuration is exposed to uncontrollable environmental stresses. These stresses are called *noise* factors. The results are hen measured in terms of *robustness* or the degree to which each combination is affected by the *noise* factor. Dr. Taguchi calls this the *signal to noise ratio*.

For example, various combinations of flour, yeast and baking soda can be baked to make the ideal loaf of bread, while the oven door is opened and closed. The result measured could be the height of the baked bread. The combination that resulted in bread loaves whose height is closest to specification, with the minimum amount of variability would be the most robust bread design. It would have the highest signal to noise ratio.

Quality Function Deployment

During the 1980's, Drs. Mizuno, Akao, Makabe and Fukahara ushered in the latest generation of Japanese quality systems. The emphasis was shifted towards the ultimate quality goal of *understanding what the customer desires* and satisfying those desires.

Quality Function Deployment (QFD) is a system for sequentially translating customer requirements into applicable product development requirements at each phase of a new product development project, while minimizing the translation losses usually inherent in such an undertaking.

It has been reported by the American Supplier Institute (1) that successful users of QFD have reported reductions in product development time which typically ranged from 1/3 to ½ of that experienced previous to the implementation of the system. This can be directly related to start-up costs of greater than 60% between 1977 (1) (when they started using QFD) and 1984.

Full implementation of QFD would require that technical staff members would assist marketers in orienting market research so as to maximize the transfer of market information into technical vernacular. The marketers would in turn review the resulting documentation to assure that the message was transferred correctly. A system of *correlation matrices* would be used to assure that <u>what</u> the customer desires is related to <u>how</u> it is to be realized and <u>how much</u> each aspect is to be quantified and emphasized. At each sequential phase the hows of the previous chart become the whats of the new one.

In this manner, customer desired are transferred into part characteristics, from there into process operations, next to production requirements, marketing and distribution plans, and finally into customer service requirements.

QFD is compatible with tends to formalize simultaneous engineering techniques which are already starting to be emphasized in our new products.

Besides helping to alleviate the major customer dissatisfiers (and competitor satisfiers!) of extended development times and high prices, QFD techniques could be used as useful adjunct to market research focused on understanding the Quality Standards (with priorities) of the market.

New Product Development Quality

Holistic quality system planning would ideally be initiated as early as possible in the new product development cycle. Heavy emphasis could rightfully be placed on the synergistic creation of functional new product development plans by both functional groups and the New Product Quality Section of the organizations quality structure.

The purpose of this section is to summarize key quality factors in the new product development process, major advances in design and customer integration by the Japanese, and to propose a synopsis of relevant functions for a new product quality section.

Key Quality Factors In the New Product Development Process

The new product development process needs to be systemized into sequential phases with a relatively formalized phase gate approval process. One of the primary elements of a holistic quality system would be for the quality department to participate in the development of this process and to assure that it is carefully documented.

The first phase in the process is typically a joint endeavor between the marketing research department and the strategic product planning group. The goal at this point is research culminating in the creation of formalized, yet flexible, market and customer requirements documentation. Market and customer needs are assessed with consideration of <u>functional requirements</u> needed to fulfill them, the time frame that they're perceived to persist and the general <u>value</u> range that they would be willing to pay to realize their desires. The competitive environment is evaluated for

121

potential 'threats,' by a "<u>Vectorial" approach</u>, which would be in terms

New Product Quality Purpose

To develop and implement quality program plans to assure that customer needs are meaningfully assessed and transferred into robust high integrity products that are readily manufacturable, testable and serviceable. The emphasis is on active involvement from product conception through ship acceptance.

Market Requirements

To satisfy our customers, we must clearly understand their present needs and anticipate their needs for the future. This must be done in a systematic manner that captures the marketing, design, and manufacturing viewpoints simultaneously and systematically. The training of these disciplines in quality function deployment techniques can be useful for the successful transfer of customer needs into production products.

Indicators:
- Customer satisfaction surveys
- Product development times
- Number of engineering changes

Requirements:
- Achieve market satisfaction in a timely manner.
- Focus on the most important needs.
- Maximize transfer of information through development phase gates.

Quality Systems Planning

The interface between the new product quality group and (A) will be established as early as possible during the product concept phase. System level SPC concepts, such as brainstorming and decision tree analyses will be used to facilitate cooperative inputs into establishing all major engineering and quality plans and documentation. Quality system planning will encompass activities from the concept phase to product ship acceptance.

Indicators:
- Approval vs. targets
- Content/thoroughness
- Clarity
- Grammar/spelling
- Implementation vs. targets

Requirements:
- Quality concept plan
- Quality milestone plan
- Manpower allocation plan

- Quality budgeting plan
- Training plans
- Vendor/component quality plans
- Inspection plans
- Test quality plans
- Phase gate transition plans

Design Qualifications

Assemblies and models need to be evaluated in terms of conformance to specifications at known levels of confidence and in correlation with program plan milestones. The specifications themselves must be accurate, reasonable, and focused towards the "Design For" concepts, including serviceability and testability. Designed experimentation and simulations may be useful in their arena. The emphasis here is on "designing in quality" as opposed to trying to sort it out by inspection.

Indicators:
- "Design for" scores
- Parametric testing
- Agency reports
- Environmental testing
- Test plan approvals
- Experimental reports
- Simulation results

Requirements:
- To plan for and implement the cost effective evaluation of sub-assemblies, engineering models and prototypes in a timely manner and to initiate corrective actions accordingly.

Reliability Assessment

The ability of products to perform over time, under stress, and in field use is the focus of reliability assessment. Based on initial assessment assemblies and products is apportioned to provide goals proportional to phases of the products life. These goals are set forth in the quality/reliability provisions document(s) and the product technical specification. Potential failure modes and their criticality must also be documented during the product development process.

Indicators:
- MTBF, MTBSC, etc
- FMECA worksheets
- PEL reports
- Field test reports

Requirements:
- Write test plans in cooperation with design engineering and new product quality.
- Complete reliability assessments, apportionments, and failure meter analyses.

- Recommend maintainability measures such as redundancy, etc.
- PEL activities
- Coordinate field problem reporting.

Vendor and Component Qualifications

The assessment of internal and external suppliers and components must be planned for during the concept stage of product development and implemented during the engineering model phase to assure the validity of prototype and pilot builds and the viability just in time implementation.

Indicators:

- Vendor surveys
- Vendor certifications
- Process capability studies
- SPC information
- Source inspections SQA
- Shipment receipts

Requirements:

- To assess the capability of vendors to supply high integrity components in a timely manner.
- To facilitate equitable corrective actions as required.
- Source/Receiving inspection plans.

126

Human Resource Systems Quality

The quality of work is directly proportional to worker motivation and job satisfaction. We must assure that the human element is considered in terms of meaningful work, skill enhancement and eventual planned transition into self managed work teams. Manufacturing engineers and production management must, in particular, be trained accordingly prior to the manufacturing pilot planning phase of new products.

Indicator:
- Job satisfaction surveys
- Absenteeism reports
- Workmanship defects
- OSHA reports
- Participation level in team projects
- Training plans and matrices

Requirements:
- To assure the manufacturing plans include provisions for: skill variety, task identity, task significance, autonomy, feedback, ergonomically sound working environment, team decision making.

Manufacturing Process Development

The elements of the manufacturing process include the documentation and implementation of the assembly processes, the introduction and maintenance of test equipment and assembly tooling, the timely and appropriate flow of acceptable and discrepant material and the reporting of quality indicators based on accept/reject criteria. (Ultimately paperless tracking systems will be employed). The use of simulations may be useful here, to predict bottlenecks, optimum inventories, and appropriate queuing systems. Planning and timing of implementation are critical factors to be mentioned by the new product group, in addition to content evaluations. Statistical methods and just in time system level concepts will be emphasized here.

Indicators:
- Completion vs. targets
- Functionality, repeatability
- Process yield, Aoq, %def.
- Late shipments, mixed lots
- Approvals vs. targets
- Simulation results

Requirements:
- Review test requirements/ plans
- Qualify test equipment
- Quality indicator plans
- Audit (process, product, lot) plans

- Review and input to process sheets, quality procedures, etc.

Part II

Psychology of Quality with Cases

The Greening of Leadership

What are the characteristics of the Green Leader? Well, that's a very good question, and one that really needs careful consideration to yield a meaningful answer.

First of all, a green leader would tend to do what's naturally best for the planet and its' inhabitants. This concept is another way of saying that the green leader would naturally facilitate the production of *right work* within the organization that she/he is in charge of.

Since sane and healthy people are naturally driven to do things that help humanity to survive and to thrive, the power of producing good things would add to the overall success of both the green leader and the organization that they lead. For example, the leader of a symphony orchestra that produces uplifting and soothing music would tend to feel good about their product and therefore be enthusiastic about the creations of their 'organization'. Conversely, a heavy metal band leader whose music facilitates to use of drugs and encourages suicide might not fell so good about their product.

This Buddhist principle of right work has deep roots in our distant past. For example, the leader of a large flock of ducks would naturally tend to do things that are good for the planet as well as for the flock. By flying south, the leader is best assuring that the ducks will have a good chance of surviving the winter. Much like in human hypnosis, the follower ducks will naturally follow the leader that they perceive to be successful; almost as if they were giving their power to the leader because that duck would increase their chances of survival better by following a successful leader than being on their own.

Now, the successful flock leader would also tend to follow the most *efficient and effective* route in the safest manner possible, given the constraints of the system. These constraints would include, geographic factors, navigational excellence, and perhaps inborn intuition of sorts, which could keep the flock out of dangerous weather and away from predators. This high quality trip would then tend to 'minimize the losses' to the society of ducks. The resulting service product would get the organization of ducks to their destination using the least amount of energy with the least amount of mishaps.

At the next level down, the duck families, analogous to the organizational department, would have to plan for the trip, be organized, focused and goal directed. The departmental manager, in the form of the duck parent, could be considered to be a leader or sorts as well, if ducklings join the flock at the proper time and location in a safe and organized manner, with due consideration for office supplies, such as food, water and the proper shelter along the way. If they sense that the overall leader is really going to help them they will naturally follow this individual.

In the human organizational situation, the department manager will tend to follow the leader that they think will help them to thrive in their organizational life. Of course, the green leader, being the archetype for excellence, will seek feedback from the lower managers, listening carefully to what is communicated and seek optimal solutions for maximum gain and minimal loss.

At the next level down, that of the individual, the green leader's influence, while filtered through the organizational ranks, will still help the individual employee to thrive. Not by chance, but by planned strategic objectives that are seamlessly turned into high quality tactics.

But how might the green leaders influence be felt so far down the ranks?

The vision of the high quality leader would first of all have to *written clearly in terms of a mission statement that is easily understood*, by both the sub manager/leaders as well as the individual employees, captures the motivational drivers of the doers and is inspirational in tone.

This high quality mission, as planned by the leadership team, would minimize the loss of the original intention of the green leader, by capturing the attention of those who will read what is stated and act on what is read if it is done right the first time.

The astute leader will assure that his/her leadership staff will create a successive hierarchy of working sub documents that will assure that the integrity of the original mission is deployed affectively to and improved continuously from each level of the organization. Quality tools such as policy deployment can be as effective the integrity of the original vision bases mission. Put simply, 'garbage in garbage out.'

To recap, *the effective green leader will minimize losses to the planet and to society by first of all producing a high quality mission based upon a vision that is good for the planet and those who live on it.*

Then, through a series of high quality communication processes, the right mix of the right tangible products and services of the highest quality will be produced using processes that produce the minimal amount of waste, if things are done right.

These communication processes themselves would produce high quality documentation that is also written using the *proper grammar and syntax*, stored using high integrity processes and protocols and

134

communicated effectively, *through the proper channels, at the right time by the right people and in the most effective manner.*

As an abbreviated example of green leadership, let's consider a new start up company that produces a new product in the form of a stress reducing rejuvenation bed, made partially from recycled material.

So then, the founder of the company gets a divine *vision* to produce a new type of bed that will make folks feel so good that they will naturally meditate and contemplate God. With no need for any other stress management tools.

The green leader of the new company will next facilitate the production of the *mission* statement. Perhaps the mission will imply that the company will --- produce the most relaxing bed, while creating the minimum amount of waste….

At the next level, *policies* might be produced which imply that designed experiments will be used to development processes which maximize adherence to specifications and therefore minimize losses to society by minimizing waste.

From these policies, clearly written *strategies* will be produced. These strategies might include training programs designed to teach the companies engineers

135

the *art and science* of experimental design. These strategies also might include teaching the manufacturing sub leaders about the importance of using ergonomically effective work spaces, with due consideration for full-spectrum lighting, proper levels of air ionization, and effective uses of color.

These high quality strategies will be used to produce *tactical* (day to day) plans that are *clearly written, are associated with realistic goals and are schedule driven*. For instance, the plant leaders might produce a *stress leadership plan* that is based on high powered hands off processes related to meditation, biofeedback and nutrition. One such plan might include stocking the cafeteria with fresh kefir and omega 3 and magnesium packed nuts such as almonds and walnuts, on a regular basis.

Other tactics might include the development of *balanced work teams* that have due consideration for autonomy, creativity, cross training and job enrichment, such as job rotations that assure that workers get to participate in the design and development of a whole product, such as the crystal and copper framed sand bed.

Top Down / Bottom Up approaches to Implementing Change

Perhaps the most daunting task associated with implementing any large scale organizational intervention is getting upper *management buy-in*, while simultaneously getting the troops to commit to the new intervention.

There are three key factors which can tend to block this top-down / bottom-up approach to leading change. First of all, those in the upper management ranks are most likely intrinsically motivated by different drivers than those in the more tactical ranks within the organizational enterprise.

For instance, the lower ranking employees are often more concerned with meeting basic physiological needs than they are with realizing their full potential as self-actualized employees. On the other hand, the higher ranking employees are more often interested in reaching more abstract, yet more significant goals, in terms of organizational impact.

According to McClellan, part of the of the reason for the disconnect is due to intrinsic motivational factors associated with the *need for power and achievement* in the higher ranking employees, which may be at odds with a stronger *drive for affiliation* in the lower ranks.

In practical terms, the corporate officer may find it much easier to facilitate a *reorganization* than the manufacturing foreman, the entry level physician or teacher or a book store clerk.

The entry level nurse may be more interested in keeping the members of the primary group, ala friends, close at hand, while the school district superintendent may be more interested in meeting or beating the budget, regardless of how many relatives he has to lay off.

According the Japanese management philosopher, Isakawa, the only way to facilitate true lasting organizational change is to meet in the middle, more *common ground*.

While many think that Isakawa's approach is that of a dreamer, the most effective strategies can only be implemented when the cooperation of the workers are matched by the enthusiastic buy-in of management.

But how is it possible to meet on common ground when upper management and their employees are sometimes from such different worlds? Let me provide an example to clarify.

As a young and idealistic engineer, I wanted to bring full-spectrum lights into a circuit board manufacturing area. Thankfully, I was successful, but I had to be a bit clever to accomplish my goal.

To be a successful *change agent*, it was necessary to appeal to the needs of people who looked at the manufacturing world from very different eyes.

At first I *hung out in the manufacturing area and got to know the employees*. I developed a questionnaire which indicated that these workers would often get headaches from the eyestrain associated with working under cool white lights.

This *data was next turned into information* that struck a cord with management. Previous studies had demonstrated that a switch from cool white lighting to full spectrum bulbs was associated with increases in productivity of as much as five percent due to the characteristics of the improved lighting that simulated natural sun light.

Since attention was being paid to the employees, the famous *Hawthorn effect* could not be entirely ruled out. However, a variety of beneficial psycho-physiological factors, including the spectral or color characteristics of the light, were claimed by many to be at play here, including the quality of the full spectrum lighting itself.

Importantly, as discussed more thoroughly in earlier chapters, the lens of the mammalian eye will become overstressed when exposed to lighting that is devoid of the beneficial near wave ultraviolet light. As a reminder, unbalanced light which is skewed towards the yellow to red part of the spectrum has been associated with increases in stress hormones and even with excessive growth of the glands that produce these chemicals; the adrenals. The excessive growth is associated with the increased demand upon the glands to produce more stress hormones.

Even packed with a bale full of supportive documentation, management wanted more proof that the lights could save the company more than it cost to re-lamp; especially since the full spectrum variety were more expensive.

By developing a designed experiment in cooperation with the corporate statistician, we eventually demonstrated a trend towards productivity increases of about 0.5 percent. While a half of a percent may seem very low at first, the result in this area alone equated to tens of thousands of dollars per annum. These profit increases were based upon a decrease in *defects in combination* with increased in productivity.

The real clincher was when an assembly line worker explained to a senior vice president that lots of folks were complaining of headaches and that a trial of the lights seemed to make things much better and *absenteeism and health care costs* were going away. When he heard that piece of advice, a check was cut the next day and the ROI was considerable!

Once the initial innovation was in place, the process of *continuous improvement* was implemented. In this case, there were some very intricate soldering processes that were improved by using a greenish hued desk lamp that made the boards appear brighter due to the physical characteristics of the human eye.

In the end, the full-spectrum ambient light, in combination with the bright light as needed, proved to be the ideal quality innovation; based upon top-down / bottoms-up communication and collaboration which leveraged their unique motivational factors while reaching a common ground. In this case, increased profits for the company.

At the time of the innovation, the US economy was struggling. Therefore, *job security* (the second rung in Maslow's simplified hierarchy of needs) was extremely important to the assembly workers. Taking sick days due to eyestrain were even unacceptable to the employees themselves, while increased healthcare costs could lead to more layoffs. At the level of upper management, the need for budgetary balance was necessary for the officers to maintain *credibility* and therefore *power*.

It is also important to consider the context within which a quality innovation will be implemented.

At an earlier time, I recommended that a lighting change be implemented in a police department in which the night crew at the front desk was also suffering from eyestrain and headaches.

While increases in productivity were difficult to imagine, let along measure, communications between the police chief and the troops resulted in a low cost innovation that yielded happier employees at minimal costs.

While safety and health cost considerations were worthy of consideration, the chief knew that the value of ethical innovations that brought about improved well being and happiness were every bit as valuable as direct ROI calculations based upon conventional P and L analysis.

In more recent times full spectrum lamps were brought into an accounting firm for evaluation. Since the ambient lighting in the room was affected by a large window, the impact was less dramatic. In fact, while some employees loved the new lights and felt less stressed, some employees didn't like the new lighting. They were used to brighter light that was skewed more towards that yellow-green part of the spectrum; since it stimulated the human eye more.

It was recommended that a type of bulb with a twist that increased surface area could increase the amount of light emitted, while not raising energy requirements. This clever *technological innovation* would pay off in many ways. Psychological innovation can often pay off in even greater ways.

In another case, ***motivational matching*** was used to launch eleven products by a three member team in a period of just over a year with superior quality than similar products in its class. Without similar consideration for these individual differences, a 10 member team could not even launch even one product in the same class in more than two years of numerous non productive and cumbersome meetings.

In this case, the team leader was sought out by upper management *do whatever it takes* to get those products out there. And that he did, to the benefit of all *stakeholders* involved.

The leaders astute boss recognized that the proposed leader was not only *driven by autonomy,* but this individual had a young family and was going to graduate school while working full time at a very demanding job.

In this case the leader's leader devised an unconventional strategy that worked like a charm. The revenue associated with this innovation increased revenue by more than a half billion dollars over the next few years. Not bad from a four billion dollar company.

Knowing that the company was in dire straights, the leader's boss told him *honestly* that if he failed that many people would lose their jobs. He also instilled *confidence* in the team leader by making it known that he trusted him and that he *knew that he could make it happen.*

To sweeten the deal, the boss told the team leader that he *only had to come to work for important meetings* and that he could do his job anywhere and any time he wanted; at the beach, in the bathroom and at 3 am if he wanted to.

This approach not only motivated that team leader to do his best, he actually put in more hours than before he was *empowered* to such a high level.

Since he knew that the team leader was highly motivated, he also wanted to be sure that he didn't burn himself out.

Contrary to the counter productive *overtime culture* so prevalent at the time, the astute boss did his best to motivate the leader to limit his hours, in very creative ways.

At the end of the work day, when he knew that the highly driven leader was on the premises, he would stop by on the way to the bathroom to complete his daily ritual of brushing his teeth at the end of the day.

In a *friendly way*, he would prompt the team leader to take a walk on nice days and to get home in time to *play with his kids* or at least get his homework done.

The team leader was very grateful to receive two promotions in one year. This reward motivated the leader even more. He worked harder than ever and would continuously improve the new product development process for future programs.

Since the company was really in dire straights financially, the boss eventually ran out of financial rewards for the team leader.

He made sure to *publicly reward* the leader whenever possible. This reward motivated the team leader even more as he rapidly rose up the steps of *Maslows' hierarchy of needs*.

It was clear to the boss that the leader was driven towards *self-actualization* and that further education and training was a cost effective way to keep the leader and the company going.

More graduate school and more seminars were on the agenda to the benefit of all. Even the team won by this approach, as the team leader would share relevant aspects of what he learned with members of the team.

The team itself was designed to be *intentional* rather than reactive in nature. One intention of the team was to keep the *top-down / bottom-up communication* system going at all costs.

By keeping middle and even upper management informed of the teams' progress, including highlighting the wins made by *staff employees*, they *bought in* to the team's *unconventional methods* of operation.

Conversely, lower level members of the *extended team*, beyond the *core team*, were on a first name basis with management at all levels throughout the enterprise.

For instance, engineering technicians would often communicate their innovative ideas for improvement directly to program development leadership, beyond the team level.

As their ideas became accepted more readily on a regular basis, their *self-esteem* would be seen growing in obvious ways. As predicted by Maslow, the increased self-esteem would and did increase *social*

146

awareness and confidence, making the interaction with management even easier than before.

The more *line and staff met on common ground*, the more they would *joke and have fun* together.

As they began to see each other more and more as *people*, rather than boss and employee, a more *lighthearted and happy* felling could be felt to the benefit of all.

While the company was still in dire straights for a while, the *mutual respect* and *participative* interaction led to even more sharing of ideas and creative expression to the benefit of all stakeholders. These benefits were even later reflected in the companies stock.

Soon thereafter, it was at the highest level in the companies' history.

Customer centric optimization

Understanding Hidden Customer Requirements

In healthcare, not paying careful attention to customer needs and requirements can lead to significant consequences, including malpractice, law suits pertaining to inappropriate behavior and even death. In fact, one of the leading causes of death in the US is considered to be the healthcare system itself. The inherent *referent* and *expert* power can lead to its own demise.

As an example, of what could go very wrong by not paying attention, let us make up a case. The astute health care leader would be wise to make up her / his scenarios in order to prevent dire results in their own organizations.

In our fictitious case, we will assume that a very influential woman was to be a patient in a busy hospital.

As part of her admissions package, she asks that she be attended to strictly by women practitioners; she wanted only vegan foods and due to her religious convictions, that she not be given certain treatments.

Further, she asks that these requirements be noted on her chart and that they be strictly enforced.

We will assume that the *quality of documentation* process was not up to snuff and that some of her requests went by the wayside and that she perceived that they were ignored. Many a limb has been wrongly amputated for similar goof ups.

Since her perceived expectations were ignored, she decides to not only ever use that hospital again; she tells her friends with similar requirements to avoid the place like the plaque and pulls back her huge donation.

The Psychology of Six Sigma, Lean & Kaizen

In a nutshell, *Six Sigma* (54) implies that there is an optimal level of quality, above which the point of diminishing returns is rapidly approached and exceeded, resulting in significant waste of resources. Below the optimal point for the product or service in question, the waste associated with poor quality is realized.

Since six sigma alone does not always tale productivity into consideration directly, *Lean* (53) processes are often integrated within Six Sigma processes to assume that time criteria is seriously considered.

For those interested in these most useful and informative systems, I highly recommend the US Army sites, including the *Lean Six Sigma* site (53) which includes significant details about these ideas without commercial bias and in a concise and useful manner.

This site provides many quality tools that may be useful for your applications from the product or service development areas into manufacturing and beyond launch stages.

Kiazen (51) is another name for *continuous improvement* which is the hallmark of most viable quality systems regardless of their applications, such as product development, manufacturing, healthcare, education, etc.

Avoiding Catastrophes

Intuition, while not always taken seriously within the domain of business, science, and technology has saved countless lives and avoided huge catastrophes. In some cases it may be prudent to follow-up with more down to earth evaluation, including second opinions. Not always, as there are times in which there is no time to think or evaluate further. In these cases, *following gut instinct* may be the only safe thing to do and natures' way of saving the day.

I once had a family member who had had exploratory surgery for a problem that had somehow just gone away. Hadda be there to understand.

By coincidence, I happened to arrive at his home early and happened to see a report of the findings of the surgery. There was something that got my attention and I had the gut feeling that I should call his doctor.

This fellow insisted that the issue I was focusing in on was a non issue and that it would never lead to anything. Another gut feeling led me to insist he write

151

down the conversation and they he never forget what I said. Even though I was being tough with him and was bold in my approach, I felt that I had to do it.

A few years later, the original problem had never returned but the issue that I had the gut feeling about killed him.

To make matters worse, the relative refused to even list to what was *intuited* because his doc did not take the potential issue seriously.

Shortly thereafter, I had a conversation with this physician who promptly told me that he I was absolutely correct, that he messed up and that he couldn't sleep at night thinking about how his negligence had led to my relatives' death.

The long term hidden costs of ignoring *intuition relating findings* were never assessed, but my *gut feeling* is that his lack of sleep and possible lack of confidence may have led to other significant problems with other patients and perhaps his personal life and that of his family.

He was not a happy camper to say the least and it appeared that this *quality event* would have impacted him, his family and his practice for a long time.

Learning to Say No to Bad Suggestions

In another scenario, let us assume that beauty salon decides to allow toenail removal because it's *the thing to do* because some other places are doing it and somebody suggested it. In reality it is one of the worse things that could be done for that business.

At the same time, let us assume that the salon had some very good hair cutters and they found that the vast majority of customers wanted hair cuts / coloring, manicures / pedicures and make up and that only a very small group wanted tow nail removal and that the vast majority of people were turned off by it.

Let's assume that one influential lady and former dedicated customer goes in for her regular haircut and finds out that her once favorite salon was now doing toe nail removal.

Before she leaves, never to return to the fancy and once well respected salon, she does get a nice hair cut, but is disgusted by a few of the things that the salon decides to do be erroneously become a full service establishment.

She happens to tell 3 of her friends about the nice hair cut she got, but at the same time tells them about some of the things going on there. Since they were shocked to say the least they even add a few things as they tell others. One lady even finds that another lady was having her toe nails removed on camera *, unknowingly, and decides to sew for millions.

Now, if not for listening to the bad suggestion to add *inappropriate services,* the salon may have benefited from the women telling three friends about the fine haircut, who in turn may have told three more about it.

It is also likely that the outraged customer will tell 10 existing or potential customers about the new services.

They being equally disgusted, tell ten others and they in turn another ten people.

In stead, assuming that the salon may have made 100 per cut / coloring, they automatically lost $2700 by the turned off customers.

This initial loss is only the tip of the iceberg for listening to real dumb suggestions.

---

* Especially with increasing violence, and for many other reasons, hidden cameras are common, especially where there is potential danger, fear of lawsuits, etc. In many cases, even employees may not know where they are and with decreasing size and cost they may be in lots of unsuspected places.

At they end of the day, 1000 potential clients are turned off and decide to go elsewhere where they feel more comfortable as they done even want to be near such things or be associated with a place that promotes such activities other turn offs.

These clients cost the foolish salon another $100,000 that has been routed to another place where people feel more comfortable.

Just thinking before and saying no to a very bad idea could have saved the salon millions over time, while retaining and obtaining more respectable customers who could have helped the salon thrive with a good reputation.

Understanding the Reengineering Process

The reengineering process is a fancy term for an organized and planned change of considerable magnitude.

Since change is inherently uncomfortable to most people, the reengineering process can be really tough on the same players that are still trying to launch high quality products concurrent with systemic organizational changes.

155

Perhaps the biggest barrier to overcome in this situation is the stress of *matrix management* during this type of change.

The old adage from the bible, *"one can not serve two masters,"* really hits home here.

In one important case, a very capable quality engineer was starting to disagree on a regular basis with his boss, who was the manager of his department.

The young man was concurrently working for the product development team, who had a different agenda that the department head.

While both bosses were committed to on time, high quality delivery, one was bent on their product development program, while the other was more concerned with reengineering processes that affected the whole company.

The young man was used to hard work, but did not want to in the middle between two bosses that had differing views. It was real tough playing the "you tell them this and that game," back and forth between the two leaders.

So, the young man trained in how to solve problems, decided to make a proposition to both managers. He asked them both to get together and to decide which person would have the most say on the young engineers performance review and how his work objectives could be structured so that each manager could have some inputs into specific aspects of the years' work load.

They *both sat down and decided* that the young man would be:

1) *focused* on the program team for the remainder of the year
2) that the department manager would re responsible for the performance review being *done on time* and submitted into the HR system
3) most important to the quality of both systems, each manager *co developed objectives*, complete with date sensitive milestones and action plans
4) each promised to have *limited input* into the objectives that other manger was responsible for

By reaching an agreement, the young man was now working as if he had one cooperative master, when in reality he still was accountable to both leaders at the same time.

By using a *participative approach*, instead of having each manager develop in isolation, based on their own agenda, the engineers' goals were *clearly documented, realistic* and *reasonable*.

By using this *relationship intervention*, a true win-win-win-win agreement was established; besides the two managers and the employee winning, the company won as well, as the *cost of conflict* is perhaps the biggest cost to any quality system.

The reduction in excessive stress for all parties resulted in establishing more productive channels in which to focus each person's *thoughts and behaviors*.

Stress Leadership

The Cost of Excessive Maladaptive Stress

By very conservative estimates, the cost of excessive maladaptive stress in the US alone is estimated to be more than a *half trillion dollars* annually. These estimates are based on a variety of factors, including, but not limited to, illness related sick days (in other words real ones), lateness and destructive behaviors, including stealing, lying and even violence, including death.

Psychosocial Factors

Until the quality system is *balanced and optimized*, the conflict between the right level of quality and reliability and the appropriate production levels can be a relentless source of stress, sometimes excessive and potentially life threatening.

However, lurking deep below the surface of stress related issues may lie the deeper causes of the most significant quality issues that any organization may encounter; intrinsic (internal) conflict.

In once knew a Chinese gentleman who had a job on an assemble line in a factory that I was associated with. Having been impressed with his witty ideas and his creative solutions to complicated problems, I asked him about his educational background.

In very rough broken English, he replied that he had a master's degree in engineering from his country, but because he could not speak English clearly that he could not get an engineering job in this country.

Since he had many family related financial obligations, he chose to work on an assembly line as the best solution to his dilemma. Since he worked long hours and had a young family, school was out of the question for him, in his opinion.

An astute management team in his area might have recognized his hidden talents (or at least listened to others' recommendation about this brilliant young man) and perhaps helped him reach his motivational destiny. Due to psychosocial factors, he was stuck at the level of *physiological need* when his intrinsic motivational level was clearly approaching *self-actualization*, or at least it was clear that he had to potential.

Adding to his stress levels was a clear sense that he felt slighted in life as many of his friends were indeed high level engineers, with great pay level, job security, and high levels of self esteem.

In a similar case, a physician from the Middle East was in the US for family reasons and ended up selling auto parts, again due to the language barrier.

Please note that life is complicated and sometimes folks end up in situations that keep them out of more serious problems or are meant to be for reasons unknown to us mere mortals.

The Neurobiology of Stress

While it is well known that some stress is necessary to get us going. This good stress, often called *Ustress*, is what gets up on cold mornings, makes us study hard for exams and even prompts to put in some extra effort and time at work when it is really needed.

Of course, what Covey calls an overtime culture () is perhaps the worse blunder any management team could make. Overtime because it's the things to do, or because it is used to impress management is very costly in terms of stress related mistakes, aggressive and other forms of deviant behavior and even workplace violence.

While the balance between ustress and optimal productivity is akin to the relationship between *Six sigma* thinking and *Lean* time and productivity processes, the human system is far more complicated that any product or service that I can think of at this time.

At first we tend to *pay attention* when external stressors are in need of our attention. The state of vigilance may be displayed in the demeanor of the factory line worker who is in the middle of a catastrophic quality issue, a physician who makes a potentially costly blunder, or the educator who makes an inappropriate comment or shows an inappropriate film in class. When the stakes are high, or when they are perceived to be, the vigilant state may turn to a potentially non productive state of paying too much attention, called *hyper vigilance.*

The hyper vigilant state, may rapidly lead to worry. In cases, worry may be an escape from experiencing or re experiencing painful emotions for the past (63).

In this case, while worry may have a useful and productive component, worry may also lead to even poorer quality than that which was caused by the original problem.

The functional and quality leadership professional in tune with the *human side of quality* will do much better by *reassuring* the worrisome employee that they are not going to lose their job, which the problem causing so much *anxiety* will be solved soon and that management is listening to them and their situation.

Active listening is a very important way to let others know that leaders are paying attention to them.

In this process, the person listening will be sure to *make eye contact with the person speaking,* will not divert their gaze on distracting influences around the room and will sometimes *repeat back the to speaker what was said.*

The repeating phase serves many functions. Not only does it assure that the person speaking is being paid attention to, the listener will also be assured that they *understand what the speaker is trying to convey.*

While *meta communication*, including *body language* can be relevant and significant, it can easily lead to mis *interpretation and miscommunication.*

Optimizing Organizational Stress

It should be clear to the reader by now that the state of balance is paramount to the state of organizational well being and associated high quality products and services.

It must also be clear that that state of balance is situational in nature and must change in alignment with external factors to make sense. Some call this situation the Tao of Quality (62).

In this paradigm, the employee functions may be considered to be analogous to five element theories in Chinese medicine; whereby employee functions may be considered to take the role of the elements of fire, wind, wood, water and earth. To achieve balance, the *yin and yang*, or feminine and masculine attributes of each element must be in harmony with each other, in ever changing environments and under ever changing conditions.

To reach a state of balance, the *seasons of change* must be seriously taken into consideration such that different solutions may apply at different levels within any system.

Important environmental designs; including those related to full spectrum lighting, negative air ionization (the good type of air found at the sea shore, in pine forests, at the beach an on mountain tops), proper ergonomics and even Feng Shui may be very indicated in high stress work spaces, like the one IVY worked in.

When visiting a US printer factory in the Southern part of the country, I was pleasantly surprised to see workers being required to take stretch and light exercise brakes twice a day.

The results in terms of increased productivity and quality levels were significant. The less tangible aspects of this type of intervention, such as an *increased sense of well being*, while not always readily measurable, were clearly working.

Adult organizations of all types can also learn from some of the *nutrition* related innovations now taking seriously in schools throughout the country.

Not only are foods with low glycemic indexes very important to maintain steady blood sugar levels, but under certain conditions could avert even the most violent of acts.

In a series of cases that happened in the 1980's, it was suggested that many violent acts, termed *going postal*, because many happen at post offices, were performed right before lunchtimes and dinner times.
Interestingly, it has been surmised that the refined white bread and coffee breakfasts prevalent in that era were believed to increase employee blood sugar significantly.

As a result of increased blood sugar levels, the pancreas will respond by excreting extra levels of insulin into the blood, typically resulting in the opposite case, which of low blood sugar levels that are self induced, sometimes called *functional hypoglycemia.*

As is well known, the low blood sugar condition could lead to a condition very much like *panic attacks common in high anxiety states.*

In another case, I was teaching a course in Industrial and Organizational psychology to a group of undergraduate psychology students, from a bio/psycho/social perspective, so I decided to integrate lots of information about important biological factors, including functional hypoglycemia.

One astute young man decided to bring some information home to his dad who had been treated for panic attacks for many years with only psychological methods.

His dad decided to eat foods that were known to keep his blood sugar more stable and low behold, his long standing panics attacks were improved more than ever and had not returned for the several years between my having his son in class and running into him at a much later date, pleasantly surprised to head of his dads' recovery.

A balanced diet, rich in the b vitamins, and the right ratio of protein, carbs and fats, including omega 3 fatty acids, magnesium, calcium and zinc, and iodine are also important when dealing with high stress situations.

Some of the hands on approaches are well known to often create more problems that they help to solve.

In fact, electronic massage chairs and other related equipment have replaced hands on approaches in many organizations.

In same cases, massage chairs where employees are fully clothed and in full view are the only type that many organizations will condone, including schools and universities.

This trend will continue in alignment with precautions against sexual harassment, law suits and rape prevention allegations.

Journaling, storytelling and a variety of cognitive approaches are rapidly finding their way into organizations of all types.

Meditation, biofeedback and music related stress management tools are well known to help human cope with highly stressful situations and are rapidly becoming the stress management of choice in organizations of all types.

Interestingly, I heard an anecdote about a woman who chanted then meditated in the work 'Hu' instead of hands on session she had booked and had somehow been canceled.

She reported that the Hu chant had worked better than any approach she had ever tried and is her stress management tool for all types of stress, including sore muscles, bones, related aches, etc.

An understanding of the power of meditation and chanting is sure to bring about a better understanding of is awesome power.

Music is also a very commonly used and powerful tool that along with meditation techniques and biofeedback have become very useful.

In some cases of depression or anxiety one side of the brain is processing information faster than the other.
In these cases special forms of meditation, biofeedback and music interventions are indicated as the wrong type can actually increase depression in some individuals.

Enhancing Human Capitol Robustness

Both being a quality leader and being an employee on a quality oriented team can be extremely stressful for all.

Perhaps the most important case that I will discuss is that of Ivy (not her real name). Ivy was a well paid and well respected assembly line worked in a fortune 500 company that was going through significant financial issues, in part because of quality related problems. This condition was extremely stressful for everyone in manufacturing area. Since she was a focal point for many quality related issues, Ivy would often leaver work, still thinking about the crisis of the day. Since I was friends with her nephew, I had first hand knowledge of her attitude and her dilemma.

One particularly stressful day on the line really appeared to get to Ivy. Her boss blamed her for not catching some important quality problems during her inspections at the same time that the bad financial state of the company was being communicated far and wide.

The next day, when I got to work, I wanted to discuss some potential solutions with Ivy. Upon inquiring about her from her nephew, I was quick to find out that she was in the hospital after having had a heart attack the night before; right after her trying day just mentioned. I was soon to find out that she was dead and that her last conversations in this life had to do with the quality issues at work.

There are a variety of extreme costs associated with the result of *poor quality related communications* in this case. These costs include, but are not limited to:

Medical expenses
Funeral expenses

Possible law suits
Recruiting costs for replacements
Associated orientation and training costs
The cost of poor feelings among others

Even if the cost of shutting the assembly line down for two days was 700,000, Ivy's' contribution towards those costs were only a fraction of overall hit, and much less than the financial liabilities mentioned..

On the other hand, the *cost of a kind and well human life is priceless.*

Many of the stress balancing innovations mentioned above are certainly indicated in high conflict areas, such as the one Ivy worked in for many years. RIP

Human Reliability

Maintaining Quality over Time

While quality may be briefly considered to be a systematic way to understand and meet or exceed customer requirements, reliability refers to the ability to maintain high quality over extended periods and or / in stressful environments.

In the case of products and services, the stresses may be mostly physical in nature; while in the case of humans, some stress may indeed be physical in nature, such as environmental and ergonomic factors that have impact on underlying physiology.

More significant, however, are psychological factors, which while they may indeed have underlying physiological consideration, there are many other factors to consider, such as motivational, situational and economic ones.

While peoples' eyesight, hearing, cognitive abilities and reactions times do tend to wear out over time, people change in many other important ways that must be carefully considered to assure high quality processes that last over time.

171

For example, let us consider the case of a person who was recruited into a manufacturing leadership program right completing a college degree, in a technical field, in which he excelled.

While he had little interest in manufacturing, he did like aspect of it and continued there but also continued his education, first in engineering, then in business.

As time progressed, this bright and capable individual also progressed in his technical and business skills.

Unfortunately, throughout his career at that organization, the gentleman was often considered to be *that guy from manufacturing*, although he always considered manufacturing to be only a stepping stone to help make him a better technical and business leader.

Robustness in Ever Changing Environments

In order to facilitate improvement and avoid negative actions, the astute *change agent* may also need a *gatekeeper* to keep track of tangible and projected change.

Without this important team approach to managing change, the change itself may blindside the unsuspecting change agent and thwart the best of intentions.

For example, I once had the honor to consult for a small company in the black forest of Germany. As part of my task, I decided to institute a training program for their quality department.

What I did not anticipate was the fluent English speaking quality leader of that group was about to take another assignment and that I had little clue as to how to implement the training program without his help.

As part of the *quality systems audit* of important company situations, I should have asked about two extremely important things:

1) Are there going to be any *anticipated reorganizations* during the time frame of the quality project in question.

2) Are there any *contingency plans* or plans to *train others* in the event of unexpected changes?

The most important team player on the project, the program manager, had a heart attack part way through the development program. No one could readily take his place.

More important than the project was this nice mans' health, but none the less, even he felt that strain of not having his own back up person.

Real dumb on my part for not asking the organizational leaders of the company in advance about *contingency plans*.

The good part was that the OEM manufacturing company changes their policies after these series of mishaps.

Mean Time between Dumb Actions

The reliability concept of time to or time between failures can be readily being applied to humans as well as products.

For example: the mean time to endoscopic perforations, complaints to the dean, rapes at salons, veterinary mishaps, wrongly diagnosed mechanical failures, corrupt police actions, peeling paint, and harassment suits by patients is just a small example of they type of human unreliability that you may find in your organizations.

You might gain much insight and avoid much pain and liability by writing down and tracking the catastrophic human failures that could lead to customer dissatisfaction, disgust, danger or violence.

Multicultural Aspects of Quality Leadership

Understanding the cultural background of significant internal and external customers is paramount to the success of the quality system. These factors may be extremely important within the quality of the healthcare process. In fact, cultural diversity could be such a powerful driver that the results could be devastating when these factors are not taken into consideration.

I once met a lady who had a child with a rare liver condition that could only be helped with a type of protein that is abundant in chicken eggs. Due to lack of consideration for the religious convictions of the family, the well meaning physician instructed the woman to feed the small child eggs for at least a short period of time.

Unfortunately, this advice led to deep conflict for the poor woman. Her spiritual teaching was deeply against the eating of meat, fish or eggs in any way or form and for any reason whatsoever.

While her maternal instincts naturally led he to try top help her child live, her religious convictions were even stronger and her baby died from the dreaded liver disease.

Had the physician been trained to better understand these powerful cultural drivers, an optimal win-win solution may have occurred instead. Had he been forewarned, it may have been possible to have used a vegetarian substitute and thereby saved the babies life.

Lack of cultural diversity has been responsible for many hidden quality issues, some of which may have been easily prevented. Conversely, an appreciation for some culturally driven factors of a positive nature could lead significant improvements in quality dynamics. Let me provide an important example.

In this case, a middle aged, well educated East Indian male had a middle management position in a fortune 500 company, working for a woman.

In his particular and specific cultural and *family background* it was inappropriate for a woman to be the boss of a man. In his case, he was obsessed by his lot and felt that he had a double whammy against him; working for a woman who was less educated than him.

Every change he could, he would chat with members of his *primary group* (friends) about how unfairly he was being treated by the company and how insulted he felt.

To make matters worse, he would in a snide way and rude manner call his boss *madam,* would spend exorbitant amounts of money on hotels and food when traveling and complain so much it was difficult to be around him. His work suffered, as he continued to contaminate those around him, in very conscious and directed ways.

The management solution to his dilemma was to leverage his very real talents and stroke his ego, by making him the manager of his own little department with his own employees, he, himself and him.

The solution worked well in some ways, but may have been significantly enhanced by providing more education and training on *gender and intellectual diversity.*

Collectivist versus Individualistic Considerations

Since this Indian gentleman was from a strong collectivist background and was therefore very deeply grounded in family traditions, and in his particular case, male dominance.

In another case, an Indian woman physician was brought up in a cultural that did not embrace the talents and capabilities of women.

In fact, it was expected that she walk behind her less educated relatives when she went home to visit. As a constant reminder of her plight, she worked in a hospital that was male dominated and in her opinion very chauvinistic in many ways.

It was not surprising that she felt a long standing loss of control and that her stress would escalate to depression; and natural response to situations in which we may feel trapped with little chance of escape. The cost of quality was significant in this case, as her *talent was wasted* on dwelling on her plight. She was often out sick, so others had to take on additional work when their schedules were already overloaded.

On the other hand, many women had significant leadership roles in her own organization.

By discussing these factors with her and telling her how woman physicians were in demand in other parts of her state that she was not aware of, and how male harassers were being handled in her organization made a huge difference. A *sense of hope* was clear in her conversation and demeanor.

Concurrently, she participated in many self help programs and became adept at *yoga, meditation, nutrition* and a variety of ways to make her robust against cultural *stress* and its associated *strain*.

179

The Asian Superstar

Many of the most highly educated and hard working employees in technical and healthcare fields come from the Asian continent and include people from Japan, India and China and many other countries.

For example, in Japan the school day and the length of the school year are not only longer than in the US, the academic rigor is significantly more difficult.

Many Japanese employees consider it an honor to work and are often dedicated way above and beyond their US counterparts.

Often the company is considered their life and they will often go to great lengths to excel in whatever they do. In some cases, their work ethic is such that they are more than occasionally found dead at their desks after having worked themselves to death; literally.

When working with the Japanese on global projects, the astute quality leader will assign team members that are *willing and able to work long hours*, often well into the night, only to start again early the next morning.

Since the Japanese will often hold short conferences, and often in their language, training in the Japanese language will certainly give US team members a competitive edge when it comes to negotiations, plans and corrective actions.

When such highly dedicated and educated employees are integrate with domestic organizations, it extremely important that they are placed in areas where they can best serve themselves as well as their organizations.
By understanding their *hobbies and interests* they may be placed on teams with others that they will best get along with. Without due consideration for the *human side of quality*, the interactions may be sub standard to say the least.

Many Asians may consider it dishonorable to display their emotions or to openly complain. Unfortunately, this holding back of emotional expression may sometimes lead to high levels of stress.

On the bright side, many Asian employees are also adept at the use of innovative and sometimes traditional stress management systems, such as meditation, Ti Chi, nutrition, and many others that may help other employees.

As these superstars are often motivated towards *self-actualization*, providing significant *educational opportunities* for these employees may simultaneously help them to fulfill their intrinsic motivational needs while helping their organizations.

In this brief case, I am going to discuss a very intelligent young man who happened to be Asian.

While he was clearly driven by a *strong work hard* ethic, and was striving to be all he could be, there was a dark side to his motivational striving. It was very clear that he was also very much driven by power and was often ruthless in his pursuit of quality.

It sometimes appeared that he had a powerful *hidden agenda* that had little to do with his concern for product integrity.

His know it all attitude and condescending mannerisms would get in the way of his capabilities in technology and quality science.

It would appear that he would often harass other technical and quality leaders to show how smart and powerful he was.

He would often argue for long periods over trivial points with anybody who disagreed with him. When he would get nowhere with other technically astute employees, he would run to management with his concerns.

After a long time feud with another technically astute leader, who he managed to turn off considerably at high costs to the organization, the other leader decided

182

that it was more important to meet this *person on a more common ground,* in this case the focal point being his need for power and control.

One day, when the Asian man arrived in the office of the person he argued with constantly, he started his typical power tactics.

This time, instead of arguing with the Asian man, the other fellow decided to *thank him* for what he had learned from him and he let him talk without reaction.

The superstar, regardless of his cultural background, got the point and backed off of his confrontational approach to a degree, to the benefit of all players involved.

The *thank you approach* can be an extremely powerful way to stop the confrontational person in their tracks.

The astute quality and functional and quality leader will learn to leverage the intellectual and technical capabilities of the superstars within their *organizational jurisdiction.*

If they are careful and treat these high achievers as partners in a *joint organizational venture,* everybody will win. One the other hand, tick off these superstars and they may up and leave; as increased confidence breeds increased self-esteem and self-efficacy, and is reciprocally related to organizational commitment.

Understanding the Hispanic Temperament

Conversely, many employees with Hispanic backgrounds are brought up to be *friendly and warm* and often value the quality of human interaction as least as much as the quality of products or services.

They often *express their emotions openly* and are more comfortable interacting at *much closer distances* than many of their US counterparts.

They may be prone to hug and / or to greet people with an extended or prolonged handshake.

The social aspect of business relationships within and outside or the organization (i.e. OEM partners, consultants, suppliers…) including a nice meal, are often important to those with a Hispanic background.

Many of these folks are very religious and do not take kindly to drinking, off color jokes or anything that they do not consider appropriate.

Gender and Leadership

According to Eagly and Johnson (60), women leaders tend to be more democratic and participative then men in similar positions.

While at it first appears that the democratic and participative management style is always, best, there are times when authoritarian management styles can work better.

For example, there are emergency situations in which a fast responding take charge leader is the only way to go. The fire and police leaders in the 911 disaster, as well as the quality of many military services, may have been compromised considerable if a more participative and democratic system was in place.

It is important to note that gender stereotypes are very often built into our unconscious minds (55) in such as way that they may compromise the integrity of any quality system.

In political psychology, it is well known that women must often overcome the conscious (56) and unconscious (55) stereotypes associated with their gender; such as feelings that they are not capable to leadership, that they nurturers geared more for domestic roles

Intellectual Diversity

According to Bassett-Jones (61) "...diversity is a recognizable source of creativity and innovation that can provide a basis for competitive advantage. On the other hand, diversity is also a cause of misunderstanding, suspicion and conflict in the workplace that can result in absenteeism, poor quality, low morale and loss of competitiveness. Firms seeking competitive advantage therefore face a paradoxical situation."

If they embrace diversity, they risk workplace conflict, and if they avoid diversity, they risk loss of competitiveness.

The advantages and disadvantages associated with workforce diversity put organizations in a position of managing a paradoxical situation. ... what its relationship with creativity and innovation might be and how the problems created by the management of diversity, creativity and innovation might be resolved.

Within the domain or organizational quality leadership, the quality of relationships is paramount successful products and services.

So, *diversity training* can be considered to be a key aspect of the quality of any organizational system.

In the new product and service development world, intellectual diversity can be the strength and the bane of any team oriented approach.

The successful quality oriented leader many assign employees based upon their motivational needs, but will naturally tend to create assignments based on intellectual and credential based stratification.

While this stratification will make for an efficient *division of labor*, it can also make for condescending attitudes and associated bitter relationships.

In order to overcome such low quality relationships, the astute leader will do her / his best to find ways to level the playing field.

Common ways to improve the quality of relationships in *outdoor experiential training* in which team members strive to solve a complicated mission, team building activities at work, including luncheons and holiday events and fun things that are safe and harmless.

When these events are family oriented, the sense of comradely among co-workers

Looking Towards the Future

Quality as a Natural Science

As psychology experts in their own rights, management experts are often exposed to a variety of psychological concepts about what drives their employees, the marketplace and society at large.

Interestingly, the most powerful driver of them all, the *drive towards homeostasis*, is the most powerful driver that I can think of, except perhaps the drive *towards dissolution and decay* when a being reaches a point when they at some level they perceive that things are hopeless.

Without the complex feed forward and feedback systems built into physiological systems, blood pressure, heart rate and liver and kidney functions would rapidly go awry. Brains without synaptic pruning of unnecessary connections and unimportant memories would require and oxygen and glucose engine in the form of a brain the size of a basketball.

This most powerful drive towards balance drives our perceptions and our goals towards *approaching* things that are in balance, such a clear complexion and fresh breath, a non-rusting car and appropriate curricular designs in educational systems, and safe and appropriate, customer driven, healthcare systems. Conversely humans tend to *avoid* and stay away from constantly flatulent people, cars that leak black oil and curricular designs or healthcare systems that could readily to in appropriate behavior and in some cases could lead to even violent behavior, even including the possibility of rape and even death in some cases.

These things are build in by nature, nurtured by our developmental environment and reinforced by academic and career paths.

Technological Innovations of Significance

The development of inexpensive imaging apparatus, such as functional MRI (FMRI) and brain wave analysis software and hardware will bring in the next generation of quality innovations.

By understanding how our nervous systems respond to relevant quality related stimuli, through watching our brains in FMRI systems of evoked potential based electroencephalographs (EEG) will take much of the subjectivity out of quality system development.

Even more subjective written instruments will be much improved by the scientific rigor now found in the natural sciences, including *cognitive science* and *psychology*.

When this evolutionary step is in place, the quality sciences will take their natural place in innovative and broad thinking schools of management within progressive university systems.

Customer driven marketing and financial systems will play their part in the far reaching evolutionary step.

Lessons from Neuromarketing

Neuromarketing is an emerging field in which our response to products is measured using sophisticated instruments from cognitive science and neuroscience.

For example, "67 people had their brains scanned while being given the "Pepsi Challenge", a blind taste test of Coca-Cola and Pepsi. Half the subjects chose Pepsi, since Pepsi tended to produce a stronger response than Coke in their brain's ventromedial prefrontal cortex, a region thought to process feelings of reward. But when the subjects were told they were drinking Coke three-quarters said that Coke tasted better. Their brain activity had also changed. The lateral prefrontal cortex, an area of the brain that scientists say governs high-level cognitive powers, and the hippocampus, an area related to memory, were now being used, indicating that the consumers were thinking about Coke and relating it to memories and other impressions. The results demonstrated that Pepsi should have half the market share, but in reality consumers are buying Coke for reasons related less to their taste preferences and more to their experience with the Coke brand." (57)

The implication for the quality systems of the future are somewhat obvious for the astute reader. Armed with an objective approach towards understanding customer desires, development teams will be able to set limits and tolerances better. They will be able to clearly understand what product or service attributes will *satisfy* and also *delight* their customers.

Equally important is a clear understanding of what may cause conflict within the brains of potential customers. Conflict may be better understood by an activation of the *cingulate gyrus*. *Disgust,* which is an important carryover from evolutionary development, may be objectified by looking at activation in the insular regions of the brain, can help us from making huge and extremely expensive mistakes.

The broad thinking leader will also consider the importance of related concepts from the domain of neuroeconomics. In this field, pricing and other economic sensitivities are treated in similar ways to those used in neuromarketing.

Since quality of the entire quality system itself is most powerfully driven by the *cost of quality* indicators, brain activation could lend considerable credence to the viability and usefulness of the quality program goals at a variety of levels..

What can we learn from Developmental Psychology?

Like it or not, the power of *beauty, cuteness and helplessness* can have a profound influence on the quality system at a variety of levels. Many serious quality issues are often overlooked due to the power of someone's appearance.

For example, the quality of the police speeding reduction system is often compromised by the leniency often provided to a good looking person, with a nice voice, who may also be cute and appear in some ways to be helpless; perhaps by crying.

At the level of the brain's *limbic system,* a beautiful appearance and nice voice are unconscious cues (real or imagined) that a potential mate is near. Cuteness on the other hard is also built into our genes (58) to help the race survive.

A small nose, large wide set eyes, and round cheeks are common characteristics among several species and early stages of development when is important to their survival to have the help of parents.

At the level of the organization, many a quality problem has slipped through the system through the power of beauty and cuteness.

In one important case, a young marketing leader was given the critical task of creating a marketing plan for a family of new products that were to be launched within a short period. She was very pretty, cute and coincidentally was about to the leave the company for a better job, so she didn't care much about the quality of what she was doing in the weeks before she was about to leave.

Unfortunately, the marketing plan was a *critical functional* deliverable that was very important to the success of the whole program that both she and the quality auditor assigned to her development program had overlooked. When the *post mortem* for the program was completed, it was found that the quality guy was letting the pretty and cute marketing team member slide by for *all the wrong reasons*. Without *beauty and cuteness profiling*, the astute quality leader would have been aware of the problem potential in the marketing area and might have looked a little closer at why this persons got away with so much at the cost of the team and other *stakeholders*.

Interestingly, the importance of understanding what *disgusts* customers may be significantly more important that what *delights* them; as we can expect that when a customer is turned off they are likely to tell about ten others, while if they are happy with something they are likely to tell only three others. In fact, *people don't even want to have any connection with things that upset of disgust them*. They don't even want them in the same organization, the same building or the same 'universe' for that matter.

In one interesting experiment, (58) ice cream that looked like feces was connected to another more pleasantly bowl by a long string. Even the connection with something that reminded them of something that disgusted them was enough to turn them away from the delightful ice cream a long distance away from the object of disgust.

Quality and the Unconscious Mind

It is well known that when people participate in groups that they tend to automatically follow leaders and that they may do things that that they normally would not if others within a group did those things.

While *leaders* may also be managers, the managerial function is focused upon the nuts and bolts of the needs of the organization. The *manager* will assure that the tasks are completed, that corrective interventions are in place and that the rules and regulations of the organization are completed in a timely and professional manner.

A leader is someone that people will tend to naturally follow without persuasion. Leaders tend to be *charismatic* and bold. They often do things that are *outside of the status quo*, are *risk takers, innovators* and *change agents*. They are perceived as strong, *powerful* and *smart*.

Leaders are usually good at public speaking, quick to make decisions and since they are innovators, they tend to deal well with ambiguity.

These characteristics may also be seen outside of the human species; in the dog pack, the bird flock and the fish school. By looking beyond the surface of these 'groups', it is readily noticed by the astute observer that their followers must at some level believe that their leader can help they in ways to better survive in domains that they might have trouble with on their own.

Unfortunately, Hitler, Manson and many suicide cult leaders were also leaders and it may be surmised that at some level of being that by following these *leaders* that the chances of survival is greater than if they were not followed.

So then, Hitler's soldiers and surgeons, Manson's groupies and Jone's poison drinkers all believed that they were doing the right thing. Or did they?

Humans tend to mimic significant, or other important people in their lives, *automatically* as an often unconscious process (55). We even have special brain cells called *mirror neurons* which are build into our nervous systems for just that reason; to help us mimic others so that we can learn to survive better.

Let's step back for a moment and look at this most important quality concept from yet another position. At some level of the brain, the leader is like the strong and capable parent. For better or for worse, the follower will do just that follow the strong and capable leader.

Keep in mind that at yet another level of the mind, the parent of the predator in the animal kingdom will learn to hunt, maim and even kill their prey in order to live.

In the organizational climate, the strong leader will have a powerful influence over their flock for better or for worse in terms of the organizations *ethics, morals and values.*

It is very important that the senior executives and the HR leaders facilitate both a *background check* and a *work history* evaluation before they empower a leader.

Leadership power is often also enhanced by their *positional power.*

As a quality leader, I was once the target of coercion by an unscrupulous VP from a company that my company had contracted to be a commodity supplier. At the time of the attempted coercion, the supplier was trying to slip by some components that had failed qualification testing.

The senior VP, attempted to *prime* (54) me for the kill, by the way he dressed, the firmness of his handshake and the strength of his words.

His little plan actually backfired. Since *power is also domain dependent*, his powerful position in his company did not carry over into the playing field of my company. The unethical VP got his company out off the list of potential suppliers, instead.

Unconscious priming could also be used for the good of the organization.

The power of *groupthink* within organizations can be the same powerful drive that may lead gang members to assault and rob their elderly victims. Conversely, the power of groups may lead to high quality spiritual choirs that uplift, motivate and heal those who listen to their songs.

In the workplace, the powerful leader must lead by example as be aware that his / her *unconscious primes* can set the tone for the day, the month, and even for the entirety of the quality program.

The power of the group will not only modify the primes of the leader; and put pressure on the *social loafer* and the *slacker*; the tone and intensions of the group are often communicated unconsciously but those with social power and influence.

There are even implications that holding a warm cup of liquid in the morning (55) may unconsciously bring on feelings of warmth and positive emotions.

Conversely, even gender or racial stereotypes are often communicated unconsciously (55) and can set the stage for significant problems within the quality system.

The empowered quality leader will do the team well by understanding these important concepts.

Lessons from Political Psychology

What the heck could political psychology have to do with quality; you might ask. Well I think it's important to understand political psychology before we can make logical connections to the humanistic evolution of holistic quality systems.

198

Political psychology has lots to do with; *how humans make choices and decisions in rational, and sometimes not so rational, ways; use and influence of power and authority; group socialization, identity, partisanship, and conformity; relationships between personality traits, cognition and emotion; conflict and attitude; communication processes and rationality in general.*

The outcomes of the political psychological processes are to facilitate the empowerment of *rational, intelligent, capable* and *ethical* leaders. These empowered leaders and the committees they govern are then supposed to develop and implement *useful policies* and processes that are meant to enhance the integrity and productivity of the groups and systems that hey help to organize.

Sound familiar? The big differences are in reality a matter of scale more than anything else. The ideas espoused by political psychology theorists are great fodder for the minds of quality leaders and those within their organizations who empower them.

In the political arena, Weston is quite correct in stating that "three things determine how people vote, in this order: their feelings towards the parties and their principles, their feelings towards the candidates, and, if they haven't decided by then, their feelings towards the candidates' policy positions." (54)

If we break this statement into generic concepts from the domain of decision sciences, we might conclude that the decision to *buy into* the quality program is an *emotional decision*, more than a cognitive one.

Employees' feelings towards the values and views and the leaders themselves within that department have much to do with how effective the quality program will be overall.

If the higher level leadership within the quality department is perceived as, for example, being micromanagement or overtime oriented, the employees within the group may develop considerable dissonance between their personal goals and that of the department.

If the quality department itself is considered to be out of alignment, the ability to gain credibility outside of the department will be lacking. On the other hand, if there is internal buy-in, the chances of promoting the values and ideas of the quality department and its' leaders are much greater.

In this case, the quality manager was a micromanager to the extreme and a nit picker like no other. He would often boast about how great a worker he was for coming to work at 5am, and he was surely dedicated, but the conflict within his department was also like none other.

One night he was overheard chastising a very experienced senior quality employee about the format of a document that he had worked real hard to finish for the tough boss. He even stayed late the night of his sons' band concert.

That was not enough for the manager, he wanted him to stay even later and redo the report. That night he was in the hospital after having suffered a heart attack.

The cost to the department was huge; especially as he a top notch well respected employee company wide and his heart attack was not taken well by many within and outside of the department.

Since he could not be readily replaced, those who tried did a shoddy job, while taking much longer to help while he was recovering from his heart attack.

While the nit picking type of manager may be perceived as inherently smart technically, they are often also perceived the type of person that might 'focus upon the details of painting the mailbox while diverting attention and resources away from painting the house.'

Since he was also perceived as caring more for unnecessary nits that for human beings, his emotional appeal was lacking to say the least.

On the other hand, some other senior managers working on the same programs were perceived as *rational decision makers* by employees within and outside of the program management teams. These same folks were *witty* and often *fun* to be around. The winning combination of *emotional and cognitive appeal* quickly brought buy-in for their values, principles and policies. Thankfully, while these true quality leaders worked outside of the quality departments per say, they were also very interested in having high quality programs; and that they did. The products in question were launched on schedule and under budget, while meeting or exceeding their quality goals.

It was the functional managers who won the vote of the engineers and other significant players, within and outside of the quality organization.

While this was a good thing in many important ways, the *wasted talent* in that of the nitpicking quality manager was a significant loss for the company. He was a highly paid employee and still had much influence within the company.

Since the nit picking type of manager may have good technical skills, and have much opportunity for improvement in their managerial skills, the decision to make this type of employee a manager rather than a technical ladder employee may also have been made with 'emotional voting' on the part of upper management, than on rational decision making processes.

From the domain of political psychology, Westen suggests that "to make their case to the public, candidates ...need to offer a story of who they are, what matters to them and what hurdles they have helped...overcome."

A more rational approach towards implementing high quality promotion processes in the form of a *structured interviewing* and *past history checks*, can be used to place higher level employees where they are best suited and can do the least amount of harm and cost the minimal amount of waste to their organizations.

These precautions are particularly important in organizations where technical employees, such as engineers, physicians, or teachers are being considered for promotion into leadership ranks. A technological leader is by no means automatically a competent or even moderately capable human leader. **This situation is perhaps the biggest downfall within quality organizations that do just that.**

The cost in terms of *seven sigma waste (i.e. allocating resources beyond the point of diminishing returns), out of time fat processes (little concern for productivity), and human waste (putting people in jobs where there is no fit while simultaneously loosing the opportunity to put them where they where they can best serve themselves and the company, can be astronomical in terms of both tangible and intangible losses to society.*

Structured interviewing may bring significant understanding into the capabilities of significant employees, especially when integrated with *biodata* about the employee. This type of information is obtained in a more *informal* manner, such as at lunch, driving from the airport or when walking to the interviewers office. (59)

Epilogue

The evolution of holistic organizational quality systems is inevitable, although the name is just a feasible candidate. As time passes, external socio-economic forces will most likely become more pronounced, causing concurrent internal organizational stresses to intensify. The organizational strain thus produced will force the organizations of the twenty second century to become more *robust,* analogous to the dense leg bones of long distance runners. The Darwinian concept of survival of the fittest will undoubtedly assure that only the most quality conscious and profitable organizations will be allowed to remain in the organizational *gene* pool. Perhaps the concept of profitability will be expanded to include the gains associated with enhancing the quality of all aspects of human life. In fact one of the primary reasons for my emphasis on the more esoteric behavioral aspects of quality, in this book, was to expound upon humanistic concepts and to hopefully plant the seeds of organizational change accordingly.

As in all times of social unrest, quality *guru's and avatars* will appear to teach much more profound quality concepts to those organizational students ready to learn and apply their teachings. Additionally, high school and college and college curriculums will grow to include the mandatory holistic quality concepts. Hopefully the newer generations of quality students will become more adept at integrating the divergent concepts promoted by the newer generations of teachers. There will be no room for Deming groupies, and exclusive Taguchi followers, in the quality oriented organizations of the future.

Quality of work life legislation in future decades will certainly undergo a process of continual improvement. By reasonable speculation the content of *quality legislation* is likely to include:

- Mandatory process efficiency legislation- aimed at reducing the waste of natural resources.
- Continuous environmental affects improvement legislation- focused on improvement *without* upper and lower compliance limits.
- Mandatory organizational stress detection and improvement systems-aimed at minimizing health care costs while maximizing employee health and happiness, in a preventative manner.
- Mandatory statistical validation for select publicly disclosed financial information. (I.e. levels of differences between annual ratio analyses give in annual reports.)

My intention was to describe select aspects of traditionally applied *quality technologies, as both a compliment and a prelude to the nontraditional offline material that was emphasized.* Please realize that only the tip of the quality systems iceberg can be discussed, in even a moderately long research paper. The science of quality is extremely broad. It can be applied to virtually all human organizational endeavors, including both the *left and right brained* varieties.

I conclude this book with mixed feelings. I feel relieved at completing one of the most time consuming projects of my life. At the same time, I feel that it will take many years before the real understanding of *humanistically* based holism will emerge within the leadership domain.

I promise you that this book will be continuously improved on a regular basis.

TO BE IMPROVED CONTINUOUSLY

Bibliography

1. American Supplier Institute; Quality Function Deployment, American Supplier Institute, 1988

2. Articles: The Origins of National Quality Month; Canadian Quality Month, ASWC Official Newsletter, February, 1990

3. Balch, David; Measuring the Quality of Work life, Quality Progress Magazine, November, 1989

4. Bernstein, Leopold; Financial Statement Analysis, Illinois RD Irwin Co., 1983, P.76-78

5. Blakw, Jan; Total Quality Control in Dutch Industry, Quality Magazine, February, 1990

6. Butters, J. Keith; Case Problems in Finance, Illinois: Irwin Publishing Co., 1987, P.8-15

7. Byars, Lloyd; Strategic Management Planning and Implementation Concepts and Cases New York: Harper & Row,1984, P. 6-16, 26-29, 74-76, 122-141, 156-159, 168-181

8. Daniels, John; International Business, Calif: Addison-Wesley P. 614-620, 648-654

9. DeCarlo, Neil; History of the Macolm Baldridge National Quality Award, Quality Progress Magazine, March, 1990

10. Fogiel, Daniel; The Statistics Problem Solver, New York: Research and Education Association, 1987, P.374-379, P.876

11. Fossum, John A.; Labor Relations, Boston; Irwin Publishers, 1989, P.33-53, 356-359

12. Freeman, Richard B.; What Do Unions Do?, New York: Basic Books, Inc., 1984

13. Grant, Eugene; Statistical Quality Control, New York: McGraw Hill 1988, P. 1-70

14. Gross, Warren; How to Grow an Organizational Culture, Personnel Magazine, September 1987

15. Hawkins, David F.; Corporate Financial Planning and Analysis, Illinois: Irwin Publishing Co., 1986, p. 206-254

16. Hughes, Philip; Lighting and The Work Environment, Duro-Test Corp., New Jersey, 1982

17. Huse, Edgar F.; Organizational Development and Change, St. Paul: West Publishing Co., 1985, P.19-28, 197-225, 236-244, 277-293

18. IDC Consulting Group; User Survey Information, 1985

19. Ireson, W. Grant; Handbook of Reliability Engineering & Management, New York: McGraw Hill, 1988, 1:13-14, 13:4-23, 15:19-27

20. Ivancevich, John; <u>Who's Liable for Stress on the Job</u>, Harvard Business Review, March/April 1985

21. Jansen, Robert; <u>Achieving Service Excellence in the Financial Services Industry</u>, National Productivity Review, Spring 1989

22. Juran, Dr. J.M.; <u>Quality Control Handbook,</u> New York: McGraw Hill Book Co., 1974, 3:1-2, 5:1-22, 8:4-31, 22:2-20, 47:4-6, 48:6-14

23. Kanter, Jerome; <u>Management Information Systems</u>, New Jersey: Prentice Hall, 1984, P.2-5, 46-49, 249-251

24. Kotler, Philip; <u>Marketing Management</u>, New Jersey: Prentice-Hall, 1984

25. Marquardt, Don; <u>Quality Auditing in Relation to International Business Strategy- What is our National Posture?</u>, ASWC Statistics Division Newsletter, 1989

26. More, Gary A.; <u>The Legal Environment of Business</u>, Cincinnati; South-Western Publishing Co., 1987, P.479-625

27. Mundel, August; <u>The Role of International Quality Standards</u>, Proceedings of the 43rd Northeast QC Council Conference, 1989

28. Myers, Michele & Gail; <u>Managing By Communication</u>, New York: McGraw Hill, 1982, P.28-29, 36-56, 142-152, 212-213, 259-264

29. Parker, Joseph; Essentials of Micro Economics, University of New Haven Press, 1988, P.21-29

30. Power, J.D.; New Car Initial Quality Survey, 1988

31. Raybac, Joseph G.; A History of American Labor, New York: The Free Press, 1966

32. Snyder, Harry: Quality Tools for the Service Sector, Proceedings of the 43rd Northeast QC Council Conference, 1989

33. Spinder, James; Quality Engineering and Quality Program Preparation and Audit, Seminar Notes, Statamatrix Institute, 1985, 1988

34. Stapleton, John; Marketing, Toronto, Coles Ltd., 1980, P.445-447, 729-754

35. Stephens, Kenneth; China's Emerging Quality Emphasis, Quality Progress Magazine, December 1989

36. Stratton, A. Donald; Kaizen and Variability, Quality Progress Magazine, April, 1990

37. Sullivan, Lawrence P.; Quality Function Deployment, Dearborn: American Supplier Institute, 1986

38. Taguchi, Dr. Genichi; Introduction to Quality Engineering, Tokyo: American Supplier Institute, 1986

39. Turban E.; <u>Fundamentals of Management Science,</u> Texas: Business Publications, 1988, P.272-292, 311, 437-447, 705-718

40. Walters, Roy W.; <u>Job Diagnostic Survey,</u> California Management Review, Summer, 1975

41. Warrick, Don D; Gardner, Don; Cougar, Dan; & Zawacki, Robert, Managing Stress in Data Processing. Datamation, April, 1985

42. Webber, Ross A.; <u>Management,</u> Illinois: Irwin Publishing, 1985, P. 36-47, 58-70, 79-85

43. Weller, Nicholas; <u>Overcoming Human and Organizational Barriers to New Technology,</u> Tappel Journal, December, 1985

44. Wolfe, Leon; <u>Lockout,</u> New York: Harper & Row, 1965, Ch. 1 & 2

45. Brealey, Richard A. & Myers, Stewart C.; <u>Principles of Corporate Finance,</u> New York: McGraw Hill, 1988, P. 207-215

46. Ben-Hori, Moshe & Levy, Haim; <u>Statistics,</u> New York: Random House, 1984, P.45-64, 256-276, 303-318, 337-339, 613-631

47. Schwartz, RM; <u>Consider the simple screw: cognitive science, quality improvement, and psychotherapy.</u> <u>J Consult Clin Psychol.</u> 1997 Dec;65(6):970-83

48. Gibbons, Mary Beth, et al; <u>Unique and common mechanisms of change across cognitive and dynamic psychotherapies</u> Journal of Consulting and Clinical Psychology, Vol 77(5), Oct, 2009. pp. 801-813.

49. Covey, Stephen R. The Seven Habits of Highly Effective People: Restoring the Character Ethic. New York: Simon and Schuster, 1989

50. Bandura, Albert; <u>Self-efficacy mechanism in human agency.</u> American Psychologist. Vol 37(2), Feb 1982, 122-147

51. Lean Six Sigma: http://www.army.mil/ArmyBTKC/focus/cpi/tools3.htm

52. Chuan, Lim Chong; <u>The TAO of Quality – Another Framework</u>. The TQM Magazine. Vol 9 (4): 250-254

53. Kaizen: en.wikipedia.org/wiki/Kaizen

54. Six Sigma: en.wikipedia.org/wiki/Six_Sigma

55. Bargh, John (ED); <u>Social Psychology and the Unconscious</u>. New York: Psychology Press, 2007

56. Weston, Drew; The Political Brain: The Role of Emotion in Deciding the Fate of the Nation. New York; Public Affairs, 2007

57. Neuromarketing: http://en.wikipedia.org/wiki/Neuromarketing

58. Keil, F.; Developmental Psychology. In Press

59. Smither, Robert, D.; The Psychology of Work and Human Performance. New York; Addison-Wesley, 1998

60. Eagly, A. and Blair Johnson; Gender and Leadership Style: A Meta Analysis. APA Psychological Bulletin, Vol. 108, no 2, 233-256, 1990

61. Bassett-Jones, Nigel; The Paradox of Diversity Management, Creativity and Innovation. Creativity and Innovation Management, Vol. 14, No. 2, pp. 169-175, June, 2005

62. Chuan, Lim Chong; The Tao of Quality: Another Framework. The TQM Magazine, Vol 9, No. 4, pp. 250-254, 1997

63. Evelyn Behar, Andrea R. Zuellig and T.D. Borkovec, Thought and imaginal activity during worry and trauma recall. Behavior Therapy Volume 36, Issue 2, Spring 2005, Pages 157-168

64. Hammer, W. C., and Smith, F. J. (1978). Work attitudes as predictors of unionization activity. Journal of Applied Psychology, 63, 415–421

65. Getman, Julius G.; Goldberg, Stephen B.; and Herman, Jeanne B. (1976) Union Representation Elections: Law and Reality. New York: Russell Sage Foundation Press

4792249R0

Made in the USA
Charleston, SC
17 March 2010